Lina,
God bless you!
Dr. ...
2 Cor

INWARD

Understanding Your True Nature in Christ

DR. WAYNE FRYE

WE WYN
PUBLISHING

VIRGINIA

Copyright © 2017 by WE WYN Publishing, LLC

WE WYN Publishing
2186 Richmond Road
Charlottesville, Virginia 22911
publisher@wewynpublishing.com

Printed in the United States of America

ISBN 978-0-692-97829-0

To my wife, Wendi
You are a Proverbs 31 woman.
Thank you for supporting me from day one.
I love you!
You are the wind beneath my wings.

And to our children, Wayne, II,
Wayden, and Wynne.
Thank you for being three of the
great joys of my life.
I love each of you!

TABLE OF CONTENTS

Introduction

The subject of RIGHTEOUSNESS is a fundamental doctrine or principle in the New Testament and as such can in no way be relegated to the background for those in the Body of Christ. Paul says in 1 Timothy 2:7: *"Whereunto I am ordained a preacher, and an apostle, (I speak the truth in Christ and lie not); teacher of the Gentiles in faith and verity."* The word verity means a true principle or belief, especially one of fundamental importance.

The Apostle Paul preached on the righteousness of God in several of his epistles. However, no other epistle majors on the theme of God's righteousness comparable to that of the Book of Romans. Paul proclaims in this letter to the Church; God's love and His forgiveness of sins. He reveals the work of Jesus to redeem man and reconcile him back to God. He shows the value of man to God and the price paid by His Dear Son Jesus to restore man to his predestined place.

His emphasis, to the Church then and now is how you should live a life and have a mode of conduct consistent with God's own righteousness; His way of being and doing right. This is the basic crux of your redemptive state, and every child of God should have an intimate and clear understanding of what it means to be the Righteousness of God in Christ Jesus. As such, it can be concluded that the principle of righteousness is of great significance and is integral in the life of every believer.

So, in the following chapters, I'll present several truths and bring out revelation on God's righteousness; what it means to the child of God to be righteous, the importance of "right and wrong thinking" and the benefits of living a life consistent with the order of God. It's my heart's desire that these truths and principles be infused in your thinking and firmly established in your heart to enable you to carry out God's plan for your life successfully.

Join me on a journey INWARD to Understand Your True Nature In Christ!

Chapter 1

A Sure Foundation

"Whoever comes to Me, and hears My sayings and does them, I will show you whom he is like (48) He is like a man building a house, who dug deep and laid the foundation on the rock. And when the flood arose, the stream beat vehemently against that house, and could not shake it, for it was founded on the rock.'"
Luke 6:47-48

Most would agree that a house should be built on a solid and strong foundation. Without it, the structure would be vulnerable and unable to withstand or stand against adversity or deemed unsound. A crack in the foundation of a house when there is inclement weather would cause the home to be damp instead of cozy and comfortable. A sense of dampness in the house would let the owner know something just isn't right. This is the same for God's people today which is the Church. You should make certain that you sure up and patch in any holes you need to patch and cover any cracks that need to be covered. Then when you step out and do what God has called you to do, or continue to do, your foundation is solid and firm. You want a foundation that is unshakable and one that cannot be moved. The Bible states in Matthew 16:18, *"And I also say to you that you are Peter, and on this rock, I will build My church, and the gates of Hades shall not prevail against it."* So, it is important that every believer has a strong foundation based on the Word of God.

Proverbs 4:1 states: *"Hear, my children, the instruction of a father, and give attention to know understanding;"* Verse seven of Proverbs 4 states, *"Wisdom is the principal thing: therefore, get wisdom: and with all thy getting get understanding."* This means that you should focus on gaining understanding. Simply put, having understanding is knowing what to do. It's the practical application of knowledge. Once there is an understanding, then you take what you know and put it into the practical application which is when results really come. It is not just what you know in your head. It is about what you know and acting on what you know. There are a lot of people that know, but still, do not have results. This will always be the case when the knowledge they possess isn't put to the practical application where they can then begin to see results in their life. Just because you know something, doesn't necessarily mean you're going to have the results of what you know. Let me illustrate. I run into people all the time where

> *Understanding is defined as a divine comprehension that enables a person to repeat something at will and get the same results.*

something happens in their life, and as I give them wisdom, they give a response of "I know, I know." Then the question becomes, "if you knew, why are you not seeing any results?" What I'm saying is this, take what you know and put it in practical application and let's see some results.

The Church should be results motivated or results driven. There's nothing wrong with being results driven. God is after results. That's why Jesus said in John 15:2, *"Every branch in Me that does not bear fruit He takes away; and every branch that bears fruit He prunes, that it may bear more fruit."* Why is this? God is after results. Don't look at this as arrogance or a lack of humility towards God. No, God is after results, and you should be too. To get the God-kind of results, you must give attention to "knowing, " and in all your getting, you must get understanding.

God's word is His wisdom. When you build your life on the word of God, you are building your life on God's wisdom, which is a sure and strong foundation. Therefore, you are assured of continual victory in each of your endeavors. No matter the storm, you will still come out of it standing because you have taken root deep in God's word. The Word of God informs and inspires every decision you make, every word you utter and how you respond to life's curve balls when they come.

The foundation of a house determines the structure that would be built on it. Any man built on the foundation of

God's word, His wisdom, can know what to expect about what "building" will be built. First Corinthians 3:9 states, *"For we are God's fellow workers; you are God's field, you are God's building."* Paul reveals in this scripture that the believer is the building of God. Therefore, once the foundation of God's word is set, the believer (building) can expect to be built into a great edifice which would not only be pleasing to God but a blessing to the Body of Christ and the world at large.

Chapter 2

The Gift of Salvation

"For by grace you have been saved through faith, and that not of yourselves; it is the gift of God,"
Ephesians 2:8

I t is the plan of God for man, you and me, to be reconciled back to Him. God was willing to risk everything for the opportunity to have fellowship with mankind. This plan was accomplished by the death, burial, and resurrection of His Son, Jesus. This selfless, obedient and loving act of Jesus provided the only way back to the Father. When you confess with your mouth and believe in your heart that God raised Jesus from the dead, you are saved that very moment. You now have eternal life. For years, the Church understood salvation only as an escape from an eternity in Hell. Few really understood the entirety and enormity of the salvation experience. God provided so much more than deliverance from eternal damnation. When you receive Jesus Christ as your Lord and Savior, four principal things happen.

First, YOU are recreated. All are born with a human spirit, but it is with a sinful nature. However, Second Corinthians 5:17 states *"Therefore, if anyone is in Christ, he is a new creation; old things have passed away; behold, all things have become new.* " When you are converted, a new spirit is created, and this takes place inwardly not in your flesh. Your old spiritual nature is changed, and you receive a new spirit that is in harmony with God. This makes it possible for you to fellowship with God on a spiritual level for eternity. Then your spirit is infused with God's Spirit (Holy Spirit) giving you an advantage over your body. At that very moment, you are no longer subject to the old sinful nature and its leadings and desires. Your spirit, the real YOU, now has the Greater One on the inside. You can now crucify the flesh by the leading and help of Holy Spirit, and walk according to the Spirit and not after the flesh (Romans 8:12).

The second major thing that takes place is your translation from darkness into the Kingdom of God. Colossians 1:9-13, states *"For this reason we also, since the day we heard it, do not cease to pray for you, and to ask that you may be filled with the knowledge of His will in all wisdom and spiritual understanding; (10) that you may walk worthy of the Lord, fully pleasing Him, being fruitful in every good work and increasing in the knowledge of God; (11) strengthened with all might, according to His glorious power, for all patience and long suffering with joy; (12) giving thanks to the Father who has qualified us to be partakers of the inheritance of the saints in the light. (13) He has delivered us from the power of darkness and conveyed us into the kingdom of the Son of His love,"* The truth revealed in verse 13 of this passage of scripture is amazing. Before the born-again experience, you were living trapped in darkness. However, through God's redemptive plan, you are no longer in the kingdom of darkness but in the Kingdom of the Son of His love. This passage of scripture also reveals the third principle thing that happens when you are born again; God delivers you from the authority of Satan. Before you were saved, he dictated how you lived your life because you were in his kingdom and you operated under his system or order. Look at Colossians 1:13 in the Amplified Bible. It states, *"[The Father] has delivered and drawn us to Himself out of control and the dominion of darkness and has transferred us into the kingdom of the Son of His love."* So, you've been taken out from under the dominion and authority of Satan and placed under the authority of God. Satan doesn't have the same control or authority over your life as a born-again child of God. The days of the devil, the enemy, taking control and doing things to you are over. Bless God! The enemy didn't take you out; you now have the power. Friend, you shouldn't run from the devil. Instead, stay submitted to God, stand flat-footed, exercise your authority, and speak to the devil and the Bible states, *"he must flee."* The devil is defeated. Jesus defeated him for you, and once you receive the salvation plan of God, you are placed in the victor's section along with Jesus himself!

The Bible reveals that he (the devil) is moving about like a roaring lion, seeking whom he *may* devour. (1 Peter 5:8)

Notice it didn't say whom he *will* devour. That means that there are a group of people that he can't devour. Therefore,

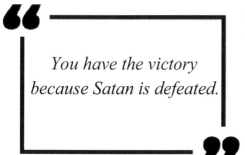

You have the victory because Satan is defeated.

you are not under his control and under his dominion any longer. You are now under the dominion of God. Now your heavenly Father has a right to speak into your life. Your heavenly Father has granted you the authority to live in victory in this life.

The fourth principle thing that happens is that God redeems you from sin and death. Sin no longer has dominion over you; you now have dominion over it. You aren't subject to the authority of the enemy and sin anymore; you can choose to do right. The grips of sin and death have been taken away from you. *"O, death where is your sting?" "O grave, where is your victory?"*(First Corinthians 15:55) Now you live free in the liberty of God!

Chapter 3

New Creation Realities

"Then God said, "Let Us make man in Our image, according to Our likeness;(27) So God created man in His own image; in the image of God He created him; male and female He created them."
Genesis 1:26a-27

M an, in Genesis 1:26 is referring to mankind, not a specific gender, male or female. God desired to make mankind in His image. He said, *"Let us…"* God the Father, Jesus and Holy Spirit; a three part being, created man. Verse 27 states, *"He created him, mankind, male and female after His likeness."* In this instance, God created man as a spirit being. He then formed the body from the dust of the ground and breathed into man the breath of life, and man became a living soul. Mankind became a three-part being after the image of God.

Man, a spirit with a soul and living in a physical body, which was created to fellowship with God for eternity was in right standing with Him. He could commune with God. There was no distance between him and God. He could live unashamedly before Him. Through Eve's transgression and

Adam's sin, man fell from his position with God. It brought about man's separation from God and resulted in every man being born with a sin nature. However, God's plan and desire for man was to triumph. The Father's love and desire to be with man, to have eternal fellowship with him and be his God would be accomplished. God would send His son; Jesus, into the earth to fulfill His plan of reconciliation. Man would be reconciled back to the Father. John 3:16 states it this way, *"For God so loved the world that He gave His only begotten Son, that whoever believes in Him should not perish but have everlasting life."*

> *It was only through the death, burial, and resurrection of Jesus Christ, that man could be reconciled to God.*

There had to be a blood sacrifice to remove man's sin and to redeem mankind. This sacrifice had to be pure and incorruptible. God, Himself, provided that sacrifice. Jesus, who knew no sin and who was divine in nature, obedient and above all else loved by His Father, was this sacrifice. Being obedient, even to death, Jesus not only took your sins, but He became sin to reunite man with God. Hebrews 2:14-17 (KJV) says, *"For as much then as the children are partakers of flesh and blood, he also himself likewise took part of the same; that through death he might destroy him that had the power of death, that is, the Devil; (15) And deliver them who through fear of death were all their lifetime subject to bondage. (16) For verily he took not on him the nature of angels, but he took on him the seed of Abraham. (17) Wherefore in all things, it behooved him to be made like unto his brethren, that he might be a merciful and faithful high priest in things pertaining to God, to make reconciliation for the sins of the people."*

God made salvation available to man and to have his right standing and position with God restored. You not only receive deliverance from the power of darkness but gain access to the promises and things of God. Your human spirit was recreated, and you also became the righteousness of God in Christ Jesus. Jesus is the way for man to become the righteousness of God for those that believe, by faith. This knowledge of righteousness is of fundamental importance to Believers. They need to abound in this knowledge and gain a better understanding of how to submit to the righteousness of God and how to conduct their lives. Paul wrote in Romans 1:16-17, *"For I am not ashamed of the gospel of Christ, for it is the power of God to salvation for everyone who believes, for the Jew first and also for the Greek. (17) For in it the righteousness of God is revealed from faith to faith; as it is written, "The just shall live by faith."* There should be a revelation of the righteousness of God. Not the righteousness of self, but the righteousness of God.

Paul said in Second Corinthians 5:17, "Therefore, *if anyone is in Christ, he is a new creation; old things have passed away; behold all things have become new."* This scripture needs to be a hallmark of your understanding of your true nature in Christ. When you accept Jesus as Lord and Savior, when you become saved, you become a new creation. That means you are a creation that has never existed before that moment. You have a new start in life. Understand the Word of God is talking about the inward nature of man. It's not referring to the physical or natural man because the outward man or physical body did not change. There may have been a change in the countenance, but the physical stature didn't change. The physical body remained the same. So, understand that a spiritual change happens.

It's important to understand that man is a spirit, which possesses a soul and lives in a body. First Thessalonians 5:23 confirms this: *"Now may the God of peace Himself sanctify you completely; and may your whole spirit, soul, and body be preserved blameless at the coming of our Lord Jesus Christ."* Therefore, when you become saved, you become brand new spiritually. This new spirit of man is what contacts God and the things of God. That means you had a spirit that was dead to God and was opposed to the things of God; however, once you become born again, your spirit becomes alive to God. You can now relate to God through a spiritual experience. The Word of God can now be understood on a spiritual level. It's no longer just an intellectual receiving from the Word of God. You are now new spiritually and can receive revelation from God. In other words, your life has been opened for

God's Word to be shown or to shine unto you; it can now be understood at a greater dimension.

God's spirit, Holy Spirit, is infused with your spirit to give you an advantage over your body. You became alive to God. The divine nature of God and your spirit are one. Your spirit now becomes more sensitive to right and wrong, good and evil and the truth and lies. Understand, the former man or your "old" spirit was trained or had a nature that desired to be satisfied. That's why, before you gave your life to Jesus, you were compelled and always drawn to sin. You were drawn to those things or areas that would cause you to miss the mark. But once you become alive to God and become a new creation, the desire to sin leaves and the desire to please God is birthed.

So, now the new spirit that you have has a desire to please God. That's why Paul says in Romans 7:18-24, *"For I know that in me (that is, in my flesh) nothing good dwells; for to will is present with me, but how to perform what is good I do not find. (19) For the good that I will do, I do not do; but the evil I will not do, that I practice. (20) Now if I do what I will not do, it is no longer I who do it, but sin that dwells in me. (21) I find then a law, that evil is present with me, the one who wills to do well. (22) For I delight in the law of God according to the inward man. (23) But I see another law in my members, warring against the law of my mind, and bringing me into captivity to the law of sin which is in my members. (24) O wretched men that I am! Who will deliver me from this body of death?"* What is Paul saying? He's saying, "I'm driven; I'm compelled by my new spirit that's alive to God. I'm compelled to do right, but my flesh is trained to do wrong. I want to do right, but my flesh keeps getting in the way. So now there's a war between my spirit and my flesh because my flesh knows how to sin, but my spirit wants to do right, and now there's a conflict." Because of your spirit now being alive to God, you are a new creation where you can now hear from God. You can understand the Word now and can be led by the Spirit of God. Old things have passed away. All things have become new. Praise God!

Paul continues in Second Corinthians 5:18 by revealing to every believer that they now have the ministry of reconciliation as well as the word of reconciliation. Verse 20 of Second Corinthians chapter 5 states, *"Now then, we are ambassadors for Christ, as though God were pleading through us: we implore you on Christ's behalf, be reconciled to God."* We'll look at this more in a later chapter, but this is just amazing. God says, now, you become representatives of Him and the only way that you can represent Him properly is that you possess His nature inwardly.

As an ambassador for Him, you need to be connected with God so He can help dictate the affairs of your life. Paul goes on to say in verse 21, *"For He made Him who knew no sin to be sin for us, that we might become the righteousness of God in Him."* Verse 21 of the Amplified Bible states, *"For our sake, He made Christ virtually to be sin who knew no sin."*

Look closely at this; here's a man, Jesus Christ, who knew no sin but was made sin. Why? So that man might be made the righteousness of God in Christ Jesus. The Amplified continues this way, *"Who knew no sin so that in and through Him, we might become endued with, viewed as being in, and examples of, the righteousness of God; what we ought to be, approve and acceptable and in right relationship with Him, by His goodness."* God took the sin of man, put it on a sinless sacrifice and then took the righteousness of a sinless man and put it upon a sinful people so they can be righteous.

This is the 'Great Exchange'. Jesus took your sin, gave you His righteousness so that now you can be viewed or be an example of the righteousness of God because you couldn't do it on your own. Jesus transferred his righteousness to you, by choosing to exchange it for your sin because He was obedient to God, not for himself, but for you to be righteous. You couldn't even get rid of sin on your own. So, if you can't get rid of sin on your own, then how can you be the righteousness of God on your own? God gets involved in your life. He literally steps on the inside of you and because He is in you,

> *You need to know the reality of your new nature in Christ and understand who you really are in God.*

then whatever is in Him comes to you. Because He's righteous, you become righteous.

You need to know Him intimately, so you can truly know who you are in Him. The whole point is to find out, to know and to understand who God is and who He has made you be. Spiritually, you get your image from your Heavenly Father. When you get this revelation, you step up in the things of God and life. God Almighty, Himself stepped in you, and He didn't leave any of His attributes out of you. He brought His holiness, His righteousness, His power, His love. Everything He has, He brought with Him!

Jesus received your sin so that you could be made the righteousness of God. Now the key word here is **MADE**. Notice it's not to become, but that you are **MADE**. That's key because there are many people still trying to become righteous when the scripture says they have been made righteous. Once you obtain an increase in knowledge as to who you are in Christ Jesus; and understand the cost or the price paid to make you the righteousness of God, in Christ Jesus; you will not only recognize the importance of having a lifestyle of righteousness but will have a greater appreciation of the love of God and your Savior Jesus Christ.

Chapter 4

Made the Righteousness of God

"For Christ is the end of the law for righteousness to everyone who believes."
Romans 10:4

I would like to share several different definitions of righteousness, but they all are of equal importance. The first definition is *a right standing with God.* When the Bible says you've been made the righteousness of God, it means that you now have a right standing with God. You are in good standing with God. When you are in a right standing with someone, you have greater access than when you don't have right standing. Righteousness is also defined as, *a good position with God.* You are not only right with Him, but you also are in a good position with Him. You are now with Him and accepted in Him.

God gives you right standing and a good position so you can have total access to Him. Let me break this down. If you are a person of excellence and you keep your car nice, straight and neat. Then someone gets into your car, and they have mud on their feet. Like that's not bad enough, they go into their backpack, and they bring out the desert from their lunch that they didn't finish. They're eating mashed chocolate cake, and it's all on their hands. The crumbs, with icing, are falling on your nice clean seats. When they get out, they don't wipe their hands; they grab the door handle with the chocolate on their hands. They get out leaving your car a mess! It doesn't take much effort to recognize and appreciate that this person most likely won't be riding in your car again or least not soon. Why? They will no longer have right standing or in a good position to get into your car. The whole idea is this; God gives you a right standing and good position with Him so you can have access to Him and all He has, no matter how messy you are.

Righteousness causes us to have rights with God. Now that you are righteous of God, you have rights. You have a right to be blessed. You have a right to be healed. You have a right to have peace. You have a right to have joy. These are not just privileges, but they are rights. For example; as a citizen of the United States in good standing with the constitution, you have a right to vote when you are above the age of 18. That's a right that you have, and no one can take that away from you, but you can make choices to cause it to be taken away from you. Some would say, "Dr. Frye, how can you say that we have a right to these things?" Well, I'm only teaching what the Bible says that you have a right to. Hebrews 6:12 (AMP) states, *"In order that you may not grow disinterested and become [spiritual] sluggards, but imitators, behaving as do those who through faith (by their leaning of the entire personality on God in Christ in absolute trust and confidence in His power, wisdom and goodness) and by practice of patient endurance and waiting are [now] inheriting the promises."* Merriam-Webster defines 'inherit' as 'to come into possession of or receive especially as a right or divine portion or to receive from an ancestor as a right or title descendible by law at the ancestor's death. The scripture you just read stated, *"Through faith and practice of patience we inherit the promises."* What promises? The promise of healing; *"who Himself bore our sins in His own body on the tree, that we, having died to sins, might live for righteousness—by whose stripes you were healed."*(1 Peter 2:24) The promise of peace; *"Peace, I leave with you, My peace, I give to you; not as the world gives do I give to you."*(John 14:27a). The promise of joy; *"I have told you these things, that my joy and delight may be in you, and that your joy and gladness may be of full measure and complete and overflowing."* (John 15:11 AMP) Righteousness makes faith, prayer, healing, joy, and peace possible.

Righteousness is also *the ability to stand in the presence of God without any sense of guilt, condemnation or inferiority.* That means, when you understand your righteousness, or that you are righteous, you can stand in God's presence and not have a sense of guilt, condemnation or inadequacy about any of your shortcomings. The blood of Jesus covers all of that. When you receive Jesus and receive His work on the cross, then His work on the cross covers you. Therefore, you can enter into the presence of God and stand before Him as if sin never existed in your life. Even if you've just made a mistake, you can go to God and enter His presence, saying, "God, please forgive me" and the blood of Jesus will cover that situation. You can have access just like you've never done anything wrong. God is awesome because when He forgives you, He doesn't even remember it. Praise God!

Next, righteousness means, you have *the very nature of God imparted to you.* What am I saying? I'm saying when you become a child of God and the righteousness of God, then God's nature is imparted you; He comes on the inside of you. So, when He comes on the inside of you, He brings His nature with Him. You now have God's DNA such that if there were a spiritual blood test, it would determine that God is your Father. Say out loud, "I HAVE THE NATURE OF GOD ON THE INSIDE OF ME!" God has chosen to put this treasure in earthen vessels so that the Excellency of the power is not of us but Him. Now shout out loud, "I HAVE THE NATURE OF ALMIGHTY ON THE INSIDE OF ME!"

The sixth and last definition of righteousness that I will discuss is, *knowing who you are in Christ.* This is essential to be successful in the things of God because when you know who you are, really know who you are, you know how to function and operate in your rights. You know how to take advantage of your privileges. I heard a story some years ago about a Pastor that had a school at his church. At one time or another, he had several of his grandchildren, if not all of them, attending the school. One of the grandchildren was misbehaving one day and was sent to the Director's office. The grandson was told, "If you don't shape up, we may have to kick you out of the school." The grandson turns and tells the Director, "You can't kick me out of this school." The Director said, "Why can't we kick you out of school?" He turned and said, "This is Big Daddy's school." The grandson understood who he was in relation to where he was. So, the grandson understood that, yes, the Director or Head of the school could make some decisions, but he was connected to the one who makes THE decisions, his Grandfather. Aka "Big Daddy."

As long as he understood his position and who he was as it relates to "Big Daddy," he understood there are some things that he was going to have privileges to. As a child of God, you should understand that you can operate the same way when you know who you are. Every child of God, including you has a right to the Blessing, Prosperity, Healing, Joy and all that God has promised and the devil can't keep it from you because it's your (Big) Daddy's promise to you. If a believer could just grasp the understanding of who they are as it relates to being a child of God. It would propel them into a different dimension in their fellowship with God. It's amazing, even in the life of our young children; we see some glimpses of their understanding of who they are as it relates to being our children. There are some things they ask for that take us by surprise or we're taken aback by them, and we wonder "Where did that come from?" When we stop and think about it, we realize it comes from them knowing who they are. They possess an uncanny knowledge that Daddy and Mommy will take care of them. It's amazing how I can tell our children something, particularly our oldest son, and they will remember it word for word. No question about it, our oldest is not going to forget it.

> *If the children of God could get to the place of truly having a child-like trust in God, the sky wouldn't even be a limit.*

If we ever want to remember something, we just tell him, and he'll remember. He doesn't forget anything. So, we'll say something and sometime later the next thing you know, he'll bring it up, and I'll answer, "What are you talking about?" He'll say, "Well you said it." "What did I say?" "You said this and then that." I'll reply, "Yeah, that's what I said alright," and so now I must follow through. It's wonderful how he has so much trust in his parents compared to believers who barely have that amount of trust in Almighty God. It could easily be said, "God you said it and that settles it!" Every believer needs to get to the place where there is a true understanding of their true nature in Christ.

Psalm 139:14 states, *"I will praise you, for I am fearfully and wonderfully made; Marvelous are your works, and that my soul knows very well."* You see, you're not just taking up space. You're not just holding on to God's unchanging hand. You're not waiting on the sweet by-

and-by until the morning comes. You should not want to 'fly away.' You've heard these lyrics before, "I'll fly away." Why would you want to sing "I'll fly away"? We need to change this way of thinking. These songs came out of a person's situation or experience. They just become perpetuated, and people just sing them even though they may not have the same experience as the person who wrote the song. When you understand who you are in Christ, who you really are, you embrace the reality that you are a child of Almighty God. This relationship with God supersedes any natural relationship that you have. Yes, you were born to natural parents, but as soon as you become a child of God, God takes over. The relationship you have with God supersedes that relationship you have with your own natural parents and anyone else.

Now, it's right and good that you have good relationships with your natural parents, because the Bible says that you ought to honor your father and mother (Ephesians 6:2). However, you need to understand that your relationship with God is more important than your relationship with your natural parents. There are times, depending on how things are set up, you can almost depend on your relationship with your natural parents more than your relationship with Almighty God. But you must understand who you are in Christ because when you truly understand who you are in Christ, you will immediately add value to yourself. I had an opportunity one time to hear a minister share on the love of

God and how the love of God is so priceless that it's free. In other words, you can't even put a price on it, so it must be free. Wow, that's amazing! Again, when you understand who you are in Christ, you ***immediately*** add value to yourself. Once you fully understand what it took for God to redeem you back to Himself, it will then help you ascribe more value to yourself. In fact, the truth is if you don't understand or have a revelation of what it took for God to redeem you back to Him, you won't have a real revelation of how valuable you are.

It's vital that know who you are in Christ. It costs God something to get you back and sometimes when you don't have to pay for something; it doesn't become as valuable as if you had paid for it. For instance, it would be easy for me to spend your money because I don't know what it cost you to get it. Now, when it comes to mine, I'll think about it a little bit more. I'll ask questions like, "Is this necessary? Do we need to have this now? Is this too much? Can we get this at a discount?" I'll deliberate. I'll make sure that if I execute this decision to spend my money, I'm going to get the best value compared to the cost that it took me to get it. But if you want to open your checkbook and wallet to someone, they may buy a whole lot of stuff and wouldn't even blink an eye. Right? See, this salvation experience is completely free for all men, although it did cost God something. Even though you didn't have a price to pay, outside of cutting off those works of the flesh, it should be valuable to you.

People can have a doctrine of suffering, and they think the doctrine of suffering is that people should always be in trouble. Always sick. Always poor, etc. That's not a true doctrine. The suffering of a child of God is having to cut the flesh off and its desires. The Bible says, allow me to paraphrase it my own way, *"when the eye is wandering, "pluck it out"; "when the hand is doing what it shouldn't be doing, "cut it off."* (Matthew 5:28-29) That sounds like suffering to me. In other words, it means, crucifies your flesh; i.e., shut it down. The next time your flesh starts screaming, you scream back, "No!" That's suffering because your flesh will talk to you. It will holler and scream, moan, cry and complain. Suffering means that you just cut it off and you allow your new inward nature to reign. It means to set your flesh down and allow your inward nature to rise. The point I'm getting across is that you didn't have to pay anything to get saved; you seemingly did not invest anything to enter this relationship with God, so it would be easy not to ascribe a whole lot of value to it. God, on the contrary, every time somebody gets born again, sees or is reminded of the price He had to pay to allow somebody to be born again. Every time God looks at you, He remembers, He had to give up His son for you. Choose to honor the gift of salvation that God extended to you.

In my early years, while I was growing up, I lived with my Grandmother. One of the ground rules she set was to prevent me from entering some rooms in the house because I was a little child. I couldn't even look like I wanted to go into some rooms. I'd just pass it and keep on going. There were rooms that I just couldn't go in. Those rooms would have furniture covered in plastic, little figurines, crystal candlesticks, candy bowls, the family Bible and all the pictures of the generations. The room stayed the same all the time. When she'd go in there, she'd pick up a figurine, dust underneath it and put it right back down. That room never changed. Why? In that room was furniture that cost more than the furniture cost in all of the other rooms combined. She protected this furniture more because of the value she had ascribed to it. So, if you were to ascribe more value to yourself based on the value that God places on you, you would not put yourself in positions to be damaged or taken advantage of, used or misused. You would say to yourself, "I'm too valuable for this, too valuable to be in this place. God paid too much for me to allow myself to be in this place. He paid too much for me to be walking around, living this kind of life. He paid too much for me to be acting this way, to be living this way, to have this condition, to have this coming out of my mouth, to have this kind of relationship. He paid too much for me."

Look at Genesis Chapter 1 again. Verse 26 and 27 states, *"Then God said, "Let Us make man in Our image, according to Our likeness; let them have dominion over the fish of the sea, over the birds of the air, and over the cattle, over all the earth and over every creeping thing that creeps on the earth." (27) So God created man in His own image; in the image of God He created him; male and female He created them."* You were made in the image and likeness of God, right? God, because you mean so much to Him, made you in His image, after His likeness. He could have chosen to make you in any image He wanted, but He chose to make you and me in His image. What does that mean? It gives you a glimpse of how important man is to God and how He feels about His man. He made man in His image and likeness, and He caused a man to be in a place of dominion.

The man was meant to run the earth and have dominion over it. You really should be living at the level where everything in this earth should be obeying you, since God said, *"Let them have dominion."* You should be in charge. God designed it so that you could rule on the earth. But Adam, who represented all mankind, did not fulfill his responsibility to dress and keep the garden as God commanded. Adam was ordained to protect it against that which was evil. His responsibility was to protect it against anything that was not like God. He instead caused the original state of man to change from a place of dominion to a fallen place. Consequently, man immediately goes to a place where he was not designed to be. That's why, even now, when things are not working right, when things are not happening right, and when things are not going the way you want, it's so uncomfortable for you. You were never designed to be in a place any lower than where God created you.

That's why you can't tolerate pressure, you can't stand being uncomfortable, and you can't tolerate sickness and disease. You can't stand it, why? You were never designed to be in it. I'll use myself as an example. I know I wasn't designed to be in large bodies of water. I can enjoy it to a certain point, however, when it gets to be too much, I can't stand it. Why? Because I was designed for land, not water; I don't have gills. Just like a fish can't stand to be out of water because it wasn't designed for it. There are some species that come out of the water, come upon a land, lay their eggs and then go back in the water. However, most fish are not designed to be out of the water; they can't stand it. I guess I wasn't designed to be in large bodies of water because I can't stand it.

You were not designed to be in trouble, distress, sickness, poverty, lack or a sinful state. You were not designed to be there. It's out of character for a child of God to be in these situations, and you can't stand it. No wonder you do everything you can to get out of it as quick as you can. There are those that even manipulate, lie, cheat and steal to get out of these places because it can't be withstood. Now, I'm not condoning these actions, but there are those that will do whatever they can to escape these circumstances.

Notice again; in Genesis, that was a man created at this place of dominion and then all of a sudden due to Adam's choice, mankind is caused to fall to a place where he is not designed to be. Adam forfeited the authority or dominion of the earth that God had given to him. Further in Genesis, chapter 1, it's revealed that Adam was designed to get the food from the earth without even sweating. You are designed to work but not sweat. Glory to God! In other words, to have 'sweatless' victory. But now, suddenly, man is in a state that requires the sweat of his brow. A state where God never intended man to be. Through the wisdom of God and obedient people that yielded themselves to God and worked with Him throughout history, He came to a place where He could release Jesus into the earth realm to remind man of God's original intent.

Once you realize your position, you will function and work on this earth just as Jesus did. When you understand that God is your Father and that He is on the inside of you and you have Holy Spirit dwelling in you, it gives you a victorious perspective. *"You are of God, little children, and have overcome them: because greater is he that is in you than he that is in the world."* (1 John 4:4)

Shout out loud, "I AM THE RIGHTEOUSNESS OF GOD IN CHRIST JESUS!"

Chapter 5

TWO KINDS OF RIGHTEOUSNESS:
Man's Righteousness

Brethren, my heart's desire and prayer to God for Israel is that they may be saved. (2) For I bear them witness that they have a zeal for God, but not according to knowledge. (3) For they being ignorant of God's righteousness, and seeking to establish their own righteousness, have not submitted to the righteousness of God.
Romans 10:1-3

Throughout history, man has attempted many ways to make himself right. He has put in all sorts of effort to make this a reality. He has continually sought material things, accolades and achievements in life all in a bid to make himself right. Several years ago, a teacher of God's word by the name of E.W. Kenyon wrote a book called 'Two Kinds of Righteousness©'. In this book, he talks about the first kind of righteousness which he calls "Man's Righteousness," a result of man's effort to make himself right, and the second kind of righteousness, which is the "Righteousness of God." While the first kind of righteousness is prevalent, it doesn't yield the same results as the righteousness of God. This kind of righteousness is called "Man's Righteousness." In Romans 10, verses 1-4 states, *"Brethren, my heart's desire and prayer to God for Israel is that they may be saved. (2) For I bear them witness that they have a zeal for God, but not according to knowledge. (3) For they being ignorant of God's righteousness, and seeking to establish their own righteousness, have not submitted to the righteousness of God. (4) For Christ is the end of the law for righteousness to everyone who believes."*

> *It is a futile attempt to make oneself right by depending on one's own ability.*

Look at verse three again. The Bible says that there are those that have a zeal of God, 'enthusiasm' for God. While people have a zeal or enthusiasm for God, that zeal or enthusiasm has not been enlightened by proper knowledge. That's why I believe Paul says that some people have a form of Godliness yet they deny the power. This is a group of people going after God with enthusiasm, but they have wrong knowledge. Look at verse 3 one more time, it tells us why they have wrong knowledge; "they are ignorant of God's righteousness." If one is ignorant of God's righteousness, they will try to establish their own righteousness outside of God.

Every effort to make yourself right by yourself will be fruitless. It won't bear the results you're looking for. Without divine help, a man by himself cannot achieve what God endeavored for him to achieve. Sure, the Bible states in Philippians 4:13, *"I can do all things through Christ which strengthens me."* However, the Bible also states, *"we can do nothing without him"* (John 15:5). So, anything you try to do without God is going to end up being futile, a waste of time and effort. There's a group of people excited about God. They're in church with their Bibles, they're participating in praise and worship, they appear as if they know something, but they're ignorant of God's righteousness, and they are going about trying to make themselves right apart from God. This is a fruitless effort because every time you endeavor to make your own self-right, you become more aware of wrong things about yourself. Paul said this, *"I will do right, but every time I will do right I end up doing something wrong."* This is because the effort to do right is being made on your own. You can't fix yourself by yourself. If you could, there wouldn't have been a need for Jesus. There wouldn't have been a need for God to go through all He went through to get you saved. He would just let you fix yourself.

While the intention of people to make themselves right is genuine, they are unable to do it themselves. The dilemma is they're trying to make themselves right because they are unaware of God's righteousness and what that means for them. They don't understand that

God has made them right already through the salvation experience. So, they continue trying to make themselves right. How many times have you run into people who are invited to church or different conferences and they respond with, "I'm not ready to go to church?" In most cases, your first response is, "What do you mean you're not ready to go church?" and they reply, "Because, I have to work some things out before I go." What is that? It's a classic example of man trying to make himself right to gain acceptance before God. They are trying to make themselves right before they go to church. They don't know and understand that God has a plan to make them right and they don't have to make themselves right. People who look to receive certain promises and benefits from God begin to listen to the lies of the devil when it seems as if it's taking too long, and begin to think, "I've done something wrong" or "I'm not worthy enough to receive from God." There is a sense of condemnation because they never seem to achieve what they believe is 'right enough' to gain God's approval. They're looking for something to do to warrant God's response or blessing, or God's love in their life. This all comes from trying to make oneself right.

Everything you receive from God you receive it because of faith. Now, of course, right living secures you to receive the promises of God. That's why God cleaned the slate from the very beginning. When you receive Jesus as your Lord and Savior and are born again, He wiped away everything that was wrong and made everything right. He understood that you had to be just and upright before Him to be confident enough to receive from Him. However, God's plan does not leave it up to you to make your self right.

Now let's look at a form of "man's righteousness" from a different viewpoint. There are those who believe that doing "good" works makes their position with God right. You may hear people say, "Well, you know, I pray all the time. I read my Bible every day." Now, let's be clear. I'm not saying you shouldn't pray and read your Bible because if you're a child of God, you should be praying and faithfully reading God's Word. But praying and reading your Bible doesn't make you more right than someone else who probably isn't. This is because rightness with God is not based on your works, but rather on the finished work of Christ. Paul elaborates on Romans 10 over in Ephesians 2:8. The Word states, *"For by grace are ye saved through faith; and that not of yourselves: it is the gift of God:"* Salvation is a gift of God. God has given you salvation freely. It's not based on what you've done or will do, but based on what Jesus has done and His love for humanity. This salvation is *"not of works, lest any man should boast."*

Paul said, *"You are saved by grace through faith, not of yourselves."* Therefore, you have only one role in the salvation experience which is your choice to believe. You choose to be saved by faith since God has already done everything else. Since you've received it, now you have a part to play because you're saved, but to receive salvation all you must do is to choose and believe to be saved. You don't have to live 90 days of sinless living while thinking that between day 1 and 90, I better not do anything wrong because if I do, I might not be able to be saved. You don't do works to become righteous; you do work *because you are righteous.* You don't pray to be right. You don't worship to be right. You don't serve God to be right. You don't obey God to be right. You don't give to be right. However, because you're right, the righteousness of God by Christ Jesus, you pray. Because you're right, you worship. Because you're right, you give. Because you're right, you serve. Because of your righteousness being secured, all you must do is receive it and walk in it. So, you're saved by grace, through faith, not of yourselves. *"Not by works lest any man should boast."*

When dealing with man's righteousness, you first need to understand that man will never be able to establish his own righteousness. Secondly, when trying to establish your own righteousness, it develops what author E.W. Kenyon refers to as a sin consciousnesses. A *sin consciousness* is a way of thinking that sin will always have dominion. It's a thought pattern of unworthiness. In other words, you have a thinking that you will never measure up. You have a mindset that 'I always do wrong'. You begin to say and pray things such as, "God, I come to you as humbly as I know how, just a lowly servant trying to please you in any way that I can." That's sin consciousness. If God has made you the righteousness of God, then you are the righteousness of God. This provides you with the ability and access to God, to stand in the very presence of God with boldness and say, "God, here I am. I might not be altogether but bless God you've made me right, and so I'm here Father for some help."

Sin consciousness will keep you separated from God instead of keeping you in union with God. This sin consciousness keeps people away from God. It will have you thinking that because you don't have everything together right now, you can't approach God for anything. It will produce in you condemning thoughts like, "I can't be in the presence of God because I don't have everything together. So, why bother trying to talk to Him? Why pray? Why worship? Why go to church? Why study? Why praise God because I'll never measure up?" All that is in consciousness. It's an attitude of unworthiness. It says, "I don't deserve it." If you weren't worthy, God would have never died for you. So, knowing the truth that He did die for you, you must be worthy. Glory to God!

Sin consciousness has a way of thinking that tries to validate the saying, "I'm a sinner saved by grace." You are not a sinner saved by grace. The truth is you're a saint that has been saved by grace. Well, Dr. Frye, I sin sometimes. That's understood because you're not perfect. Listen, don't waste time dwelling on your shortcomings and condemning yourself. Go before God, confess and repent of the sin, receive your forgiveness (1 John 1:9) and move forward in the things of God. Just because you sin one time, doesn't make you a sinner.

With a sin consciousness, you go after the promises of God with the thought of, "Have I done enough to merit this? Have I done enough to deserve this? If I could just get enough people to pray for me or with me, I can get me an answer." These questions all come from having sin consciousness. As the righteousness of God, you should be confident in prayer because the Bible states, *"the effectual, fervent prayer of a righteous man avails much—makes tremendous power available, dynamic in its working." (James 5:16b)*

If no one else prays for you, remember that you can pray for yourself with confidence because you are in right standing with God and you are the righteousness of God. You have a right to go to God and ask for and to receive what you need. A prayer chain is good but isn't needed. You can pray and ask God for yourself knowing that He hears and will answer your prayer. Sometimes, the prevailing question is, "Who could I get to pray for me?" or the prevailing thought is that I need to call my Pastor or his wife to pray for me. Now, let me add balance to this. There's nothing wrong with you calling for the elders because the Bible says you can. However, don't call for the elders of the church for everything. There's nothing wrong with having prayer partners, however, what I'm saying is if what you are thinking or conscious of is that you can't get this yourself, then you do not fully understand the righteousness of God.

Second Corinthians 1:20 teaches that *"all the promises of God in Him are yes, and in Him Amen, unto the glory of God by us."* That means that He already said yes to it, even before you asked for it. If you had to do something to deserve it, how can He say "yes" before you ask? You must come to the realization, that you can't do enough, on your own, to warrant or be worthy of the things of God. But with God, He both loves and covers you. When you get connected with Jesus, you then receive the promises of God. You didn't get it on your own merit but received it because of who you are connected to.

This sin consciousness thinking is still prevalent among God's people although God has made them righteous through Jesus. It should be rooted out because it can become a stronghold. When you are dealing with a stronghold in your thinking, it causes you to function in a certain way, and there are times you don't even know why you function that way. It's simply because there is a mindset or a way of thinking in you that causes you to act in a certain way. There can be a stronghold of sin consciousness just like there may be a stronghold as it relates to a poverty mentality. A person can have a poverty mentality yet have plenty of money in the bank and still live as though they don't have anything. A poverty mentality causes one to act in a particular way unaware. If a sin consciousness is still your way of thinking you'll act in certain ways and there are particular things you wouldn't dare think about

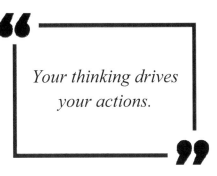

Your thinking drives your actions.

asking. Let me jar your thinking here. Why are you considering what you have done? It's not about your works. It's about what has been done for you.

I can recall another time in my childhood when I would stare out of the car window as my mother drove through different neighborhoods throughout the town where we lived. I would think to myself, as I looked at things in amazement, things that seemed so far out of my reach, "Oh, maybe one day" or "Oh, I'll never be able to get to that place." That was a negative thought pattern I was building up over time. Think about it for a minute; your environment causes you to have a certain thinking based on where you are. Now, if you don't allow yourself to be exposed to new things and new information, you will get stuck at a level, and you'll continue to live at that level when you don't need to. You can have a sin conscious mindset and be able to receive more but not receive more, not because God doesn't want you to have it but because you won't allow yourself to have it based on the way you are thinking.

You need to embrace what God has done for you and say what He says about you. Decide today to see yourself as God sees you and to call yourself the righteousness of God in Christ Jesus. Yes, there may be things you need to work on and things that need to be changed. I understand that you walk around with the flesh, but you can choose not to live according to the flesh, and choose to live according to the Spirit. It's a choice that you make. Decide to agree with God and allow Him to develop you from the inside out.

Paul taught this truth in Romans 3:9-26, *"What then? Are we better than they? Not at all. For we have previously charged both Jews and Greeks that they are all under sin. 10 As it is written: "There is none righteous, no, not one; (11) There is none who understands; There is no one who seeks after God. (12) They have all turned aside; They have together become unprofitable; There is none who does good, no, not one." (13) "Their throat is an open tomb; with their tongues, they have practiced deceit"; "The poison of asps is under their lips"; (14) "Whose mouth is full of cursing and bitterness." (15) "Their feet are swift to shed blood; (16) Destruction and misery are in their ways; (17) And the way of peace they have not known." (18) "There is no fear of God before their eyes." (19) Now we know that whatever the law says, it says to those who are under the law, that every mouth may be stopped, and the entire world may become guilty before God. (20) Therefore by the deeds of the law; no flesh will be justified in His sight, for by the law is the knowledge of sin. (21) But now the righteousness of God apart from the law is revealed, being witnessed by the Law and the Prophets, (22) even the righteousness of God, through faith in Jesus Christ, to all and on all who believe. For there is no difference; (23) for all have sinned and fall short of the glory of God, (24) being justified freely by His grace through the redemption that is in Christ Jesus, (25) whom God set forth as a propitiation by His blood, through faith, to demonstrate His righteousness, because in His forbearance God had passed over the sins that were previously committed, (26) to demonstrate at present His righteousness, that He might be just and the justifier of the one who has faith in Jesus."*

He has justified you. Glory to God! You may have sinned and come short of the glory of God, but now, you've been justified. You can look back at your life, the life you had before Jesus, and relate to it being a life of sin. I'm not exalting sin, but I'm just pointing out that before Jesus, it can be said, "I had a life of sin." Yet, when you are born again and begin to gain knowledge and understanding that you were freely justified, you are now no longer equated like someone without God. Now, you've become the righteousness of God, and now the righteousness of God has covered and taken care of the life of sin. Yes, at one time, You sinned and fell short of the glory, but because you received the righteousness of God sin no longer has dominion over you. You are right with God. You have a right standing with God. You can come into his presence like you have done nothing wrong at all. Why? Not because of what you did but because of what He did. The truth is that God and Jesus took care of sin. As a result, you no longer live under the banner of, "All have sinned and come short of the Glory of God." Now, you live under the banner of the righteousness of God. Shout out loud, "I AM THE RIGHTEOUSNESS OF GOD IN CHRIST JESUS!"

Well, you may be asking, "Dr. Frye, how do we get rid of this sin consciousness?" Roman 12:1-2 teaches, *"I beseech you, therefore, brethren, by the mercies of God, that you present your bodies a living sacrifice, holy, acceptable unto God, which is your reasonable service. And be not conformed to this world: but be transformed by the renewing of your mind, that you may prove what that good is, and acceptable and perfect, will of God."* This scripture reveals the life-changing truth that you are transformed by the renewing of your mind. What's known about sin consciousness is that it is resident in your thinking; thinking that you're not good enough; you're always going to do wrong; you'll never be right with God. If you're going to change your sin consciousness, then you must change your thinking! You've got to begin thinking differently, and the way you think differently is to renew your mind.

For example, some people have attended a church all their lives, and all they've ever heard about was a sin. Sunday after Sunday and in mid-week Bible study, everything was about sin and how a man falls short of the glory of God. Well, that's what they're going to have faith for since it's what preached all the time. They were told information on what was wrong and what not to do but didn't receive information on how to change for the better. So, if a person doesn't know any better how they can do any better? The mind must be renewed. The mind is so sophisticated that it is designed to determine or receive as truth, the first or the initial information that it receives regarding a subject. What does this mean? When you learn something new for the first time, your mind grabs it or holds on to this initial information and labels it as truth. When new information is presented, the mind then goes into the mode to either reject, debate or not receive the newer information about that subject. This happens in spiritual and natural things, principles and promises.

Let's say that you hear that prayer should be some emotional and sensational experience and if you don't feel a certain something when you pray then your prayer just goes to the ceiling and bounce back to you. However, that's not true; the Bible just simply says you should pray the Word of God. You can pray the Word of God whether you feel it or not. On purpose, set yourself to hear the truth and allow the truth to uproot all things that are contrary to the Word of God.

Hebrews chapter 4 reveals that the Word of God is quick (alive) and powerful, sharper than any two-edged sword and can divide between the soul and spirit. The Word of God is the only thing that can penetrate your wrong thinking. You need to understand that wrong thinking is keeping you away from the presence, the power and the goodness of God. Believing and trusting in God's Word takes you to a higher level of faith. Second Timothy 3:16 states, *"All scripture is given by the inspiration of God..."* God inspired a man to write the Word. It continues with. *"all scripture is profitable for doctrine."* Doctrine is the *established order of God.* So, whenever you see doctrine, that's the order of God; and God is a God of order. Verse 16 continues with, *"All scripture is for reproof."* Reprove is simply *dismantling of your thinking.* All believers came into the relationship with God with a certain mindset or thinking based on the past, based on experiences and based on environment. Come on, you can admit it! The fact is you came to God with thinking that was not correct because your thinking was not renewed automatically when your spirit was reborn. That's why there were mindsets and thoughts you have before you get saved, remaining after you get saved. The verse concludes with, *"all scripture is profitable for instruction in righteousness."*

> *The Word of God is profitable, beneficial, advantageous to change and renew your mind that you may be perfect, completely equipped for all good works.*

Verse 17 states of the same chapter state, *"That the man of God may be perfect, thoroughly furnished unto all good works."*

As you see, to get rid of this sin consciousness, you have to renew your mind. You must develop a new way of thinking, and the way to do this is to let God's Word in. You must continually let God's Word in until you begin to think like God's Word, as opposed to the way you thought before. You need to continually hear the Word of God's righteousness, His redemptive power and your position with God. When you hear God's Word repeatedly, it then flushes out your old way of thinking. It's done with this subject of righteousness, just like it's done for healing and health, faith, love, etc. Your mind must be changed to think about yourself the way God thinks about you. Every child of God is on top, but might not be living on top. Spiritually, you're in a place of dominion. A place of authority. The Kingdom of God is the only place where everyone in the Kingdom is a king. In other Kingdoms, there are kings, queens, princes, other rulers, and servants. Not in the Kingdom of God. All are Kings! Sadly, some people pull back from God in this life waiting until they get to heaven with an understanding that when they get there all the things that made them 'unworthy' will be done away with and finally they'll be received and accepted by God. This isn't what the Bible teaches us. The Bible says you're accepted by God just as much now as you will be when you stand before God in heaven. Ephesians 1:6 states, *"To the praise of the glory of his grace, wherein he hath made us accepted in the beloved."*

God cannot do anything else to receive you more than what He's already done, and you cannot do anything else besides receiving Jesus to be received by God. God releases and opens everything to you the moment you get saved. The moment you say, "Yes," to Jesus, you're in God's presence, and He's in you!

Shout out loud, "I AM THE RIGHTEOUSNESS OF GOD IN CHRIST JESUS!"

Chapter 6

TWO KINDS OF RIGHTEOUSNESS:
The Righteousness of God

But what does it say? "The word is near you, in your mouth and in your heart" (that is, the word of faith which we preach): (9) that if you confess with your mouth the Lord Jesus and believe in your heart that God has raised Him from the dead, you will be saved. (10) For with the heart, one believes unto righteousness, and with the mouth, confession is made unto salvation.
Romans 10:8-10

The above scripture outlines how you get saved. You believe in your heart that God raised Jesus from the dead and confess the lordship of Jesus. Salvation is not obtained by only attending church. No different than a person becoming a car if they walk into a garage. It's more than going to church. You must believe in your heart and confess. Verse 10 states, *"For with the heart one believes unto righteousness; and with the mouth, confession is made unto salvation."* Notice, with the heart you believe. So, to really experience this righteousness of God, it will require you to believe; this is your part. When it comes to the promises of God, everything is received by faith and faith includes believing. Your actions will always line up with what you believe.

If someone consistently tells you something opposite to who you really are and you sincerely believe it, then your belief in what is being said will over-ride the real you, that true inward nature. *"As a man is as he thinks in his heart, so is he."* With the heart, man believes unto righteousness. So, if, in your heart, you believe that you are unrighteous or unworthy, you will then begin to act and behave based on how you believe not based on how you've been made.

The point I'm making is that you've been made the righteousness of God in Christ Jesus, but if you choose not to believe it, your unbelief can override how God made us. Let's take the story of Jesus when He went into His own hometown to minister to them and their needs. Afterwards, Jesus said *"no prophet is accepted in his own country,"* and then the scripture states, *"there He could do no mighty works, because of their unbelief."* You must understand that your belief system is so powerful that it could override truths from God's Word. That's why it is so important that you develop your belief system on the truth of God's Word and change your belief system to what God is saying in Scripture.

It is important for you to know and understand the revelation of having been made the righteousness of God. You must believe in your heart that you have been made the righteousness of God that you've been redeemed from darkness and the power of sin and death has been broken. For you to walk in and experience this righteousness, you must first believe it. Once you receive this revelation, no one can take it away.

Romans 5:12-16 states, *"Therefore, just as through one man sin entered the world, and death through sin, and thus deaths plead to all men, because all sinned— (13) (For until the law sin was in the world, but sin is not imputed when there is no law. (14) Nevertheless, death reigned from Adam to Moses, even over those who had not sinned according to the likeness of the transgression of Adam, who is a type of Him who was to come. (15) But the gift is not like the offense. For if by the one man's offense many died, much more the grace of God and the gift by the grace of the one Man, Jesus Christ, abounded to many. (16) And the gift is not like that which came through the one who sinned. For the judgment which came from one offense resulted in condemnation, but the gift which came from many offenses resulted in justification."*

Let's look at these scriptures. The Bible lets us know that Adam represented all humanity. When Adam sinned, he allowed sin into the world. As a result, sin was then imputed to every single human born from that point on. Even a baby, a newborn baby, though they haven't had an opportunity to sin at all, the sin of Adam is imputed to them. This may be difficult to grasp or handle, but Adam is the representation of all mankind. Just as Adam's transgression opened the door to sin and death, also by one man, the second Adam,

Jesus Christ, through His work, permitted the justification for that sin. Look at Verse 17 again. Adam let the offense in, but Jesus' work took care of the offense and then released the gift called righteousness. Through Adam, we all were a part of that sin nature, but when a man or woman gives their heart to Jesus, the work of Jesus covers that offense, justifies them from sin, and they are no longer a sinner. Dr. Frye, did you say I'm no longer a sinner? Yes, you are no longer a sinner if you have received Christ by believing in His finished works for you and confessing His Lordship. You were once under sin, but, glory to God you are no longer under sin because of the work of Jesus. You are the righteousness of God in Christ Jesus!

I cannot stress it enough how important it is for you to believe that you are the righteousness of God through the born-again experience. However, that's not all. Next, you now need to receive this gift of righteousness. What does it mean to receive the righteousness of God? It simply means to accept, to embrace and to take hold of it. Your mind might be bringing back to your memory all the wrong things you have done to negate this truth; however, you must accept who you are in Christ Jesus. Why? It's because what Jesus has done for you is more powerful than what your mind can fathom. Some have memories that dig deep and every time a similar experience occurs; it digs a little deeper into their thinking. That's why it sometimes takes longer to change the way you think. You want to think differently, but it's such a challenge because some things are deeply rooted.

In some cases, self-forgiveness is almost impossible because of the severity of the situation. Again, these are strongholds in your thinking. You must develop your heart to believe and accept that you have now been made the righteousness of God no matter what your mind is saying.

You've got to take hold of it and when you do, don't let it go. Take the stance that no one is going to take it from you. Your situation is not going to take it from you. People are not going to take it from you. The opinions of others will not take it from you. Past mistakes are not going to take it from you. You have this righteousness, and you're not going to let it go. Be confident in this gift of God. You can't earn a gift; you can't work for a gift, you simply receive it. Look at it in a different light. When you've worked for something or when you've met all the qualifications, and then something is released to you, it's not a sense of a gift. When you receive a gift, it's because someone wanted to bless you with something out of their own goodness.

God loves giving gifts. Think about it for a moment. He gave you Jesus. He gave you righteousness. He gave you salvation, peace, joy, love, etc. God is the ultimate gift giver. But, the fact is many

> *Here's the truth: Jesus paid the price. He shed His blood for you. As a result, you can freely receive what God has freely given!*

people are not receiving the gift because of thinking that they do not measure up or deserve His goodness. Hallelujah!

Ask yourself this question. How will I respond when I'm asking God for something, and the devil says, "What do you think you're doing?" He follows that question with the statement, "You don't deserve that!" What is your response going to be? Is your response going to be "Oh yeah, you're right." "I forgot about that." or "Gosh, what am I doing?"

If you've embraced the righteousness of God, it doesn't matter what the enemy is telling you. John 8 states that the devil is a liar and the father of lies. You've been spending too much time believing him, more than you've been believing God. Remember, First John 1:9 is the provision to be cleaned after any shortcoming that you find yourself in. *"If you confess your sins, He is faithful and just to forgive you and to cleanse you from all unrighteousness."* Again, righteousness is who you are. You must retrain yourself, based on the understanding of your true nature in Christ.

A lot of Christians are doing things because they don't know who they are. Once you know who you truly are, then do not continue doing the things that you were doing before understanding this important revelation. Stop making excuses as excuses are essentially the crutch of the uncommitted. If you use excuses, you just want to lean on the crutch which means you are not walking on your full weight and full responsibility. Once you know and understand the truth, you can't use an excuse. When you hear the truth from the word, you become responsible to do the Word actively. God will hold you accountable for those things that you've heard. Once you know better, you should do better.

Just think about that! God is not going to continue to allow a whole lot of unworthiness talk. Holy Spirit will begin checking you. What I mean is this: on the inside, you'll get a check such as "That's not right. I shouldn't be talking like this anymore." That's Holy Spirit ministering to you now that you know. Part of the ministry of Holy Spirit is to bring things back to your remembrance which He has shared with you. So now, when you do something contrary to what you've heard, it's His responsibility to remind you, to check you.

Don't look for Holy Spirit to forcibly check you. He's going to check you gently and He knows how to do it to get your attention. However, you need to be sensitive enough to respond to that check. The more you override it, the less sensitive you'll be to it. A person's heart, their spirit, can become callused. I'll use this illustration. I grew up with a group of folks that wouldn't wear any shoes. They wouldn't even wear any shoes when they came outside. This continued until they got to the point that they could run on a gravel road with no shoes on. On the contrary, my mother made sure I had shoes on when I went out of the house. So I always had shoes on. One day, I thought I could be like them and not wear shoes. There was a small concrete stoop as you came out the door of our house and stepping out there barefoot was fine. But when I stepped on the gravel road, I said, "Aah, aah, ooh, aah, let me put some shoes on!" Here they are walking around, running sprints and racing each other with no shoes on. The bottom of their feet looked tough and hard. Shoes probably wouldn't have agreed with them anyway. What happened? Their continual walking on those sharper objects caused their feet to build up a resistance to the gravel. Their feet began to grow layers of skin over layers of skin, over layers of skin. To my one layer of skin, they might have had four, five layers of skin.

What am I saying? You can do that same thing spiritually. Holy Spirit can try to minister to you, but if you keep resisting it, you put layer after layer over your heart until you can no longer receive the ministry of the Spirit. You become numb to the leading and speaking of the Lord. The Lord may be speaking to you, but you can't hear it clearly because you've numbed yourself by consistently resisting and resisting. You will eventually get to the point where you can't hear anything from God. You may find yourself doing things on your own and calling it God when you haven't heard from God in a long time because you've built up a resistance to the Word of God.

But, if you just give God a little crack, His Word is so powerful and so sharp that it will begin chipping away the

INWARD: Understanding Your True Nature In Christ

callused areas of your heart to allow the truth to change you from the inside out. As a result, you will become as sensitive to the Spirit of God as you were as a young baby.

Righteousness is legally yours! Why is this important? If something is legally yours, then no one can take that from you. The devil cannot take it from you. Circumstances can't take it from you. Situations can't take it from you; no one can take it from you if it is legally yours. It's common for people to think that righteousness can become lost. On the contrary, a person doesn't lose righteousness, however, they may lose the benefits of righteousness. Friend, you can't lose your righteousness! For instance, the same is true as it relates to your citizenship in the United States. As a US Citizen, you can lose your benefits of being a citizen of the United States, but not citizenship itself. If you do something to break the law, then some of the rights and privileges that come along with being a citizen of the United States may be taken away from you, but, you're still a citizen. It's the same with righteousness; it's legally yours. However, your actions can cause you to miss out on some of the benefits, but it does not make you unrighteous. Again, look at Second Corinthians 5:21. It states, *"For he has made him to be sin for us, who knew no sin; that we might be made the righteousness of God in him."* The work of Jesus secured righteousness legally because a payment had to be made for you to obtain righteousness. If go back to the beginning, in the Garden of Eden, when Adam sinned and Eve was deceived, you see that both fell from their place of grace and they hid themselves from God. This lets you know that whenever we fall from a place where God placed you, a penalty is given and a price must be paid. That's why the Bible says the wages of sin is death. Death is the compensation for sin. Therefore a payment needs to be made to satisfy the penalty.

Jesus paid the price for you to become righteous. God chose to place the sin of an imperfect world upon a perfect, sinless man, to make payment for a sinful world. Jesus, who the Bible says was tempted with all temptations as common to man, yet without sin, was sent of God to pay the price for a sinful world. To become sin for a sinful people. Why? A price had to be paid for you to be righteous legally. If that price hadn't been paid, then the enemy could rightfully accuse you before God. Because Jesus paid the price, he can't accuse you of being unrighteous since you're not righteous based on what you've done; you're righteous because of what Jesus has done. When Jesus died, Jesus not only died physically; He also died spiritually. He had to die physically because He had to take the penalty for sin that was meant for man. He had to take it upon himself to pay that price. When the Bible says God placed sin upon Jesus, that's when He died spiritually. While hanging on the cross, Jesus said, *"Father why have you forsaken me?"* This was the very first time that Jesus was ever separated from God. That separation came about when the sin of the world, was upon His life. God is holy and can't abide with sin. God literally had to turn His face away from Jesus.

The good news is when Jesus descended into hell, He took sin with Him and conquered it once and for all and left it there. When He rose again, He rose without sin upon Him. Jesus defeated sin in hell! God was then able to receive Him back to himself since He no longer had sin upon Him. Now, when God looks at you, He looks at you through the finished work and the Blood of Jesus Christ. The price, Jesus Christ, has secured righteousness so that God can always say you are the righteousness of God in Christ Jesus.

Remember, Jesus died both spiritually and physically. He defeated sin and death, which is a representation of the spiritual and physical part of your life, in hell. That's why when you become born again, born of God, you die to your old way and your old self and it's the last time you must die. Glory to God! Your spirit is going to live with God for eternity. Death for a child of God is simply a transfer of location.

The next fact about the righteousness of God is this: it is by faith and not by works. Romans 3:21-22 states, *"But now the righteousness of God apart from the law is revealed, being witnessed by the Law and the Prophets, (22) even the righteousness of God, through faith in Jesus Christ, to all and on all who believe. For there is no difference;"* We see very clearly from verse 22 that the righteousness of God is by faith. *Faith* is defined as believing in and acting upon the revelation of God's word. If you believe you're the righteousness of God, your actions should then lineup with that belief. Not the way you feel, not by what other people have said about you, but by the way you believe.

The Bible says your righteousness is by faith, therefore act as if you're righteous even if you don't feel like it. This is a challenge for some Christians. For some, when they miss the mark or fall short in the things of God, they choose to run away from God instead of believing by faith they are the righteousness of God and running to Him for help. Instead of yielding to the natural tendency, which is running away from God or blaming it on someone else, your faith needs to override the flesh. Running to God, you should say, "Father I've missed the mark. I'm running to you as the righteousness of God in Christ Jesus, and I need your help. I can't do this on my own. Father, I'm coming to you, the throne of grace. I missed the mark, but I know you will help me."

It takes faith to do that when your flesh is saying the opposite of what you believe: "You can't go to God now, you just lied. You can't go to God now, you just cheated." "You can't go to God!" But, your faith in your heart overrides how you feel, and you go to God anyway. He will receive you. He will speak to you. He will minister to you and send people across your path to help you line up and make adjustments in those areas so you won't keep missing the mark. So, it's truly a mistake if you want to stay away from God. Mature Christians become mature only with the help of God. There wouldn't be a need for Jesus, a savior, a cross or a resurrection if a man could do it by themselves.

Look at what Romans 4:1-3 states, *"What then shall we say that Abraham our father has found according to the flesh? (2) For if Abraham was justified by works, he has something to boast about, but not before God. (3) For what does the Scripture say? "Abraham believed God, and it was accounted to him for righteousness."* Verse 3 said when Abraham chose to believe God and to have faith; it was accounted to him for righteousness. Abraham never became the righteousness of God; it was only accounted to Him to be righteous. For Abraham, it's almost like it was a coat of righteousness placed upon him, but for you, it's more than a coat, it's your true nature in Christ. If you do or don't have a coat on, you are still the righteousness of God in Christ Jesus. Verse 5 continues to state, *"But to him who does not work but believes on Him who justifies the ungodly, his faith is accounted for righteousness,"* Let's look at these same verses in the God's Word translation beginning with verse one...

"(1) What can we say that we have discovered about our ancestor Abraham? (2) If Abraham had God's approval because of something he did, he would have had a reason to brag. But he could not brag to God about it. (3) What does Scripture say? "Abraham believed God, and that faith was regarded as the basis of Abraham's approval by God." (4) When people work, their pay is not regarded as a gift but something they have earned. (5) However, when people don't work but believe God, the one who approves ungodly people, their faith is regarded as the basis of God's approval."

Scripture tells us that righteousness is not based on what you do to earn it; it is based on what He has done for you to receive it as a gift. You must believe this! Your belief in God's righteousness is sealed by the blood of Jesus. You must believe that the Blood of Jesus and the sacrifice of Jesus was enough for you to become the righteousness of God. This is the truth regardless of your past, your present and what you may do in the future.

Now, let me bring some balance to this. I don't want to confuse you, and I certainly don't want you to be confused in thinking that you can do whatever you want to do since you're the righteousness of God. I must make sure I pause here. Thinking that you're always righteous, which is true, can sometimes be used as an excuse by someone that is trying to misuse the grace of God or manipulate the system of God. While the Bible does say that you are the righteousness of God and that you can't lose your righteousness, know that when you deliberately abuse the grace of God and neglect the order of God, you short-circuit the benefits of your righteousness. You will be the righteousness of God living like you're unrighteous.

A saved person living unrighteous, which is confusing to others, might end up being a stumbling block to someone coming to the Lord. Many times, people ask the question, "How can a person be saved when they're still doing what I see them doing? They can't be saved!" What they're doing is acting out of character. People are hearing them say one thing but seeing them do something else. So, what people do is say, "They aren't saved!" instead of saying "They're a carnal Christian that has not been renewed." Yes, an unrenewed carnal Christian. However, if that person truly accepted Jesus as their Lord and Savior they are saved but their choices are now displaying something that they're not. When a born-again person chooses to live in the flesh, it means they're carnal. Saved but carnal. (1 Corinthians 1:3)

Philippians 3:9 states, *"And be found in him, not having my own righteousness, which is the law but that which is through the faith of Christ the righteousness which is of God by faith:"* Look at what the scripture is saying. The scripture is very clearly saying that the righteousness of God comes by faith. Comes with what? By FAITH! In other words, you step into it. You walk into your righteousness or your state of righteousness by faith, and this should really be understood since everything you receive from God is received by faith.

All the promises of God are by faith. Faith saves you. You're filled with the Spirit by faith. You're healed by faith. You're blessed by faith. You have peace of faith. You have joy in faith. You walk in your righteousness by faith. You parent by faith. Your marriage functions by faith. You're glad to be single by faith. Glory to God!

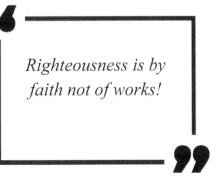

Righteousness is by faith not of works!

Please understand that you cannot live by feelings. For the simple reason that feelings may take you to a place where you don't need to be. That's why they are called emotions; energy in motion. Emotions always change—you don't ever want to build your life on something that's always changing. You want to build your life on a firm foundation, and I haven't found a firmer foundation than the Word of the Living God.

God cares for you, but He doesn't care how you feel. Remember, God is moved by faith, not by feelings. How you feel doesn't change the Word or the promises of God. You need to live based on the firm foundation of the Word and then control your emotions.

Shout out loud, "I AM THE RIGHTEOUSNESS OF GOD IN CHRIST JESUS!"

Chapter 7

Benefits of God's Righteousness: Part I

"Bless the Lord, O my soul; And all that is within me, bless His holy name! (2) Bless the Lord, O my soul, and forget not all His benefits:"
Psalm 103:1-2

Obedience to the Word of God has benefits. Walking in love has benefits. Giving has benefits. Doing what God says to do certainly has benefits. God is a giver, and He always includes great benefits to those who choose to walk and live in His way and His Word. Receiving and becoming the righteousness of God certainly comes with its benefits.

Access to God's Throne and Presence

Once you become the righteousness of God in Christ Jesus, you have every right to enter God's presence anytime that you desire—and when you do, God receives you every single time! There is not a single time when God will turn away one of His children. Not one time! Hebrews 4:16 states, *"Let us, therefore, come boldly to the throne of grace that we may obtain mercy and find grace to help in time of need."* Boldly means fearlessly and confidently.

You can confidently go into the presence of God because of your position with God. This confidence comes when you know who you are in Christ. In life, you learn who you can go to and who you're more confident in going to based on the relationship that you have with that person. For example, if you need some money you know you're going to be more confident asking your best friend than a complete stranger. Why is that? Based on the relationship, you understand you and your best friend should have a good position with one another. Even if they don't have the money to give you, that doesn't do anything to your confidence because of the relationship. But a person that you just met, they don't know you, and you don't know them. Therefore, you would be less confident in approaching them with any request because no relationship has been established. Your relationship with God should be the strongest relationship you have with anything and anyone else on this planet. There should be no one that you're closer to than God. Let me tell you why. If you're closer to someone other than God, then you will put the needs, the wants, desires, and requests of that person before God. When you have a closer relationship with your spouse than with God, you will obey your spouse before you obey God. Unfortunately, people have placed relationships with people, places and things above their relationship with God. When the people, places, and things call, they start running — but when God calls, they hesitate. Bless God, when God calls you should drop everything and ask, "Father, what is it that you desire?" You shouldn't let people get in the way of God. You need to put first things first — seek God first in everything. As long as you live nothing should get between you and God!

Let's look at verses 1 and 2 of Psalm 15. It states, *"Lord, who may abide in your tabernacle?" "Who may dwell in your holy hill?* Verse 2 answers these questions; *"He who walks uprightly, And works righteousness, And speaks the truth in his heart;"* Tabernacle is another word for presence. The Bible says the person that would dwell in the presence of God on His Holy Hill is the one that walks uprightly, the one that works righteousness. Righteousness now gives you the privilege of being in the presence of God. Friend, everything you need is in the presence of God. You can be in God's presence right now. You can enter His presence while driving, on your job or in your home. Some would ask the question, "How do I get in the presence of God?" The Word teaches us to enter His gates with thanksgiving and to come into His courts with praise!

In Psalm 16 verse 11 it states, *"You will show me the path of life; In Your presence is the fullness of joy; At Your right hand are pleasures forever more."* The Bible says that in God's presence there is fullness. Now, it says fullness of joy, but if you understand anything about God, it's that God gives all of Himself. He doesn't just give parts of himself. This scripture only references the fullness of joy, but I have personally come to realize that in His presence is the fullness of whatever you need. If it is joy, you can get the fullness of that. If it is peace, you can get the fullness of peace. If it is knowledge, understanding, and wisdom, you can get the fullness of that as well. With God, He brings the fullness of everything. Scripture reveals that the joy of the Lord is your strength. You should then understand that in the presence of the Lord, there is the fullness of joy and if that joy provides strength, then being in the presence of God will cause you to be strengthened. When things are happening externally, it is important to stay in the presence of God. It is important to stay close to God since in His presence there is the fullness of the joy which is your strength.

If you are going to stand and have fortitude, stamina, and endurance in this life for God, you should habitually be in His presence. You must learn how to be in His presence on a regular basis — not just run to Him when you're in trouble or when things are going wrong. No, you need to make it a way of life. No matter what you're doing, where you are or what you're dealing with, you can enter His presence. Every believer should make it a practice to walk with God every single day.

What I'm saying is this: walking with God, is an acknowledgment of God's presence. It's an acknowledgment of, "God is with me, and God is in me." Walking with that acknowledgement helps allow you to tap into whatever you need when you need it. There are times during the day when you may need the wisdom of God, or the peace of God or you may need the knowledge of God.

If you make it a practice of walking with God, those things are available all the time. You can be out on your routine at your job and yet still walk in the presence of God even though you are unable to be on your knees or lay prostrate. There's nothing wrong with getting on your knees or being prostrate but, the focus should be on training yourself to always be in the presence of God, not having a certain posture or position.

Let's take a minute to look at Ephesians 2 beginning with verse 11: *"Therefore remember that you, once Gentiles in the flesh—who are called Uncircumcision by what is called the Circumcision made in the flesh by hands— (12) that at that time you were without Christ, being aliens from the commonwealth of Israel and strangers from the covenants of promise, having no hope and without God in the world."* Look at that. There was a time in your life where you were alien to the promises of God. You were a stranger to the covenant. You were really living life with no hope. The scripture says, living with no hope is living without God. The enemy has deceived the minds of people not allowing them to see their need for God. They think they can do it on their own. But without God, you're in a place of no hope. But now let's look at verse 13, it states: *"But now in Christ Jesus, you who once were far off have been brought near by the blood of Christ."*

The Blood, shed by Jesus for mankind has allowed you to be close to God. One of the reasons why He shed His

Blood was so that the blood could cover your shortcomings and sins. Just think about it; Almighty God, the God of Heaven and earth, the God who created everything, wants you and I to be close to Him — and not only does He want us to be close to Him, He has made a way for us to be close to Him. Verse 14 continues, *"For He Himself is our peace, who had made both one, and has broken down the middle wall of separation,"* When Jesus shed His blood on the cross, when He said "It is finished", when He said, "The work is done", the temple veil was rent. That dividing wall that kept us from God was rent into two pieces. Glory to God! Now, there's no more separation between you and God. Now, you can have access to God and be close to God since you have received the plan of salvation. He didn't have to do what He did, but due to His love for mankind and His desire for you to be next to Him caused the wall of separation to be removed. Hebrews 9 confirms this and tells us that Jesus went into the Holy of Holies, once and for all, to shed his Blood on the mercy seat so that your blood wouldn't have to be shed anymore. He paid the ultimate price so that you, me and everybody else that is born again can have a relationship, fellowship, access and be close to God.

I want you to think about this; God is with you! God is in you and desires to fellowship with you—and not only that, He made away for you to spend time with Him. It's like having a close friend that you haven't seen in a long time. A close friend that happened to move away and you wanted to spend time with them so much that you paid their airfare, hotel bill, and all their expenses to have them come and spend time with you. All they had to do was participate in the plan you had set up, and they can be close to you. That's what God has done. God has paid the price. God has set the plan for you. All you must do is participate in what He has set up for you, and you can be close to Him. There is no reason why a child of God, you or I, should be walking away from God at any time. There should not be a place or a time in your life where you even sense that you're far from God. All you need to do is just thank and praise Him, and you can be right in His presence. Some people say, "I feel like God is not near." How can anyone feel like God is not near when He has paid for and has made way a for you to be always close to Him? The only reason why God feels far away is because of what you have done. God doesn't move. He is the Lord that changes not. He always remains the same. You and I are the ones that move back and forth. If you just draw nigh unto Him, He will draw nigh unto you. Therefore, you should always have constant communion with Him.

God will speak to you, lead you and guide you through a still small voice, giving you instructions throughout the day. He will, with a still small voice, encourage you by Holy Spirit. He will, with a still small voice, strengthen, lead and guide you in the affairs of life because you have fellowship with Him. As a child of God, you have free access to God. The door is always open. There is direct and consistent access to God all the time.

Confidence in Your Daily Walk

Once you understand that you have the nature of God on the inside of you and you know who you are in Christ, it gives you confidence in your daily walk. In other words, you should have a greater level of confidence in life knowing who you are in Christ. Knowing that you are the righteousness of God, you should be more confident than when you didn't understand who you were. There is a zeal and passion that comes along with this revelation of knowing who you are in Christ.

Confidence in God empowers you. It energizes you. It strengthens you. It's confidence in God that makes it possible to accomplish any and everything God sets forth for you to do. It's confidence that makes it possible to achieve whatever God wants you to achieve. It allows you to exist in a state of a firm trust. If you are confident that a natural person will come to your aid in the time of need, how much more should you be confident that Almighty God will come to your side or sustain you in a time of need?

> *Confidence in God drives out fear, doubt, anxiety, and worry.*

God has made the promise that He will never leave you, nor forsake you and that is because we are the righteousness of God. In fact, the more time you spend with God in His presence, the greater your reassurance is that God will come to your aid; hence, the need for you to spend more time with Him. Think about this, why wouldn't God come to your aid? God will always defend the righteous. Why wouldn't God come to meet your need? Why wouldn't God do something on your behalf? Why wouldn't He? You are the righteousness of God, His child, part of His family and His heritage. David testifies in Psalm 37:25 saying, *"I have been young, and now am old; yet, I have not seen the righteous forsaken, Nor his descendants begging bread."*

When you know who you are in Christ, it brings a sense of confidence that you have victory. No matter what it looks like, you're going to win! You can believe God for something and be confident in the integrity of His word and His person. Ephesians 1:3 states, *"Blessed be the God and Father of our Lord Jesus Christ, who has blessed us with every spiritual blessing in the heavenly places in Christ,"* You've been blessed with all spiritual blessings. Praise God! You are already blessed. Verse 4 continues to state, *"just as He chose us in Him before the foundation of the world, that we should be holy and without blame before Him in love,"* This sounds like righteousness because it says you're going to be holy before Him. Remember one of the definitions of righteousness is to 'have a right standing with God.' Look at verses 5 and 6. *"Having predestined us to adoption as sons by Jesus Christ to Himself, according to the good pleasure of His will, (6) to the praise of the glory of His grace, by which He made us accepted in the Beloved..."*

You are accepted by God. Now, if God accepts you, it really doesn't matter if people reject you. Before the foundation of the world, God wanted us to be holy before Him and accepted by Him. Acceptance brings confidence! I'll illustrate it this way. A group of kids would get together on the playground to play football or some other sport and someone yells, "Who wants to play? Who wants to play?" Before you know it, everyone responds, "Me, I want to play, I want to play!" Everybody starts to line up, and the team captains start picking the kids they want on their team. For every person that gets picked in front of you, your confidence goes down, and it is almost shattered when you are the last one to get picked. My point is this; it boosts your confidence when someone accepts you. If you really knew and understood that you are accepted by God Almighty, how much confidence would that give you? Think about it. The one who is Holy, the one who is without blemish, the one without mistake has accepted you! Shouldn't that give you the confidence to rise and say, "If God believes I can do it, I believe I can do it!"

You are accepted in the beloved which means you will never be cast out by God. God will always receive you! The Amplified translation of Ephesians 2:8 states, *"We are God's own handiwork (His workmanship)."* You are fearfully and wonderfully made in the image and likeness of God. What confidence should that give you! God could have made anything like Him, but He chose you and I to be like Him. You are His craftsmanship, and there is nobody like you. God made you uniquely the way He wanted you to be for His purpose and His design in the earth.

There are even more benefits when you have confidence in God. First, you'll have a greater level of spiritual growth. You'll believe, embrace and trust His Word more which will equate to greater spiritual growth. When you become confident in His Word, then you are more likely to do His Word. People grow by doing the Word and by doing the Word it causes changes to manifest. You really can't grow in the Word without doing the Word. You can memorize all the Scriptures, but memorization doesn't equate to growth. There are some that know what to do and still are not doing what they know. Really, growth comes through change and when something grows, it changes. You only grow through doing the Word of God, not just knowing the Word of God. That's why James 1:22 states, *"Be ye hearers and doers of the Word..."* Doers of the Word are blessed in what they do.

You will also have greater personal achievements, when you have confidence in God. Any goals that you've set because of your in confidence in God should be easier to attain because you understand you're not doing it by yourself. You don't have to be limited to only what you can do. The creator of the universe is working with you.

Confidence in God will give you greater peace in your life. Confidence equates to peace. You can rest in God; no cares and no worries because you understand that God is always working on your behalf. The last benefit of confidence I will mention is a greater or more powerful impact on the lives of others. As you're praying for others with confidence in God, there's a greater opportunity for them to be impacted by your prayers. When you're sharing the Word of God with somebody, and you have confidence in the Word that you are sharing, there's a much greater opportunity for that person to be ministered to.

This confidence that comes from knowing your true nature in Christ is designed to aid you in all areas of your life. Do not allow situations, circumstances, the enemy or anyone else cause you to step back from this truth.

Shout out loud, "I AM THE RIGHTEOUSNESS OF GOD IN CHRIST JESUS!"

Chapter 8

Be Strong and of Good Courage

"Be strong and of good courage, do not fear nor be afraid of them; for the Lord your God, He is the One who goes with you. He will not leave you nor forsake you."
Deuteronomy 31:6

As a child of God, you should have confidence in God alone; doing this will produce a strong confidence in yourself. Joshua 1:8 states, *"This Book of the Law shall not depart from your mouth, but you shall meditate in it day and night, that you may observe to do according to all that is written in it. For then you will make your way prosperous, and then you will have success."* Verse 9 goes on to say, *"Have not I commanded thee? Be strong and of a good courage. Be not afraid neither be thou dismayed for the Lord thy God is with you wherever you go."* It's humbling to know that wherever you are, the Lord is with you. And, once you recognize His presence, you can be strong and have good courage. As a result, you can exude some confidence in your life—*courage* is simply boldness. You are to be confident in God, knowing that God supports you. If you're going to operate in the Word or do the Word, be confident that the Word will come to pass.

Sometimes, I find that Christians get discouraged, meaning they have a lack of boldness. As a child of God, discouragement is out of character. That's why you're so uncomfortable in places of discouragement, depression or confusion. It's not your nature as a child of God. Why? Simply put, because you are born of the Most High God. He is your Father, and the Word says He will stick closer to you than a brother and He will never leave or forsake you. Once you're out of character long enough, you no longer know how to conduct yourself properly. Unfortunately, you may go back to what the world has taught you since it's so easy to revert to what you are used to doing. Until you've continued in doing the things of God long enough and trained yourself, this is what will happen. Instead, you should just stand firm in doing the things of God. Regrettably, most do not stay over in the new arena long enough to gain the confidence necessary. They allow discouragement to come in or they lack boldness in that arena when change does not happen fast enough. This causes people to slip back into an old pattern of living, and try to disguise it by saying, "Well, that is just who I am."

When you decide to stand firm and walk with confidence and boldness, even if you must stand alone, don't give up your commitment to change. Before long, God will raise up some people to come alongside you and encourage you and be a friend to you, when you need that sort of company the most. Even if you must stand by yourself for a time, God will soon place you in the company of people that are going in the same direction and will speak into your life, undergird and support you.

Discouragement

There are several reasons why a Believer gets discouraged. First, note that discouragement comes from the enemy. The devil seeks out to discourage whoever he can. He does this through thoughts, smokescreens, challenges and by making things difficult. His goal is to derail you; get you off-course. God has laid out a track or plan for you, and your responsibility is to stay on track. However, the devil uses whoever and whatever he can in an attempt to cause you to be fed up enough to throw in the towel and walk away from the very thing that's designed to take your life to a whole other dimension.

Secondly, discouragement comes when your plan doesn't work the way you want it to work. For instance, you may want somebody in your life to change and when that person doesn't—you may get discouraged. You devised a plan for that person to change based on what you thought was right and when it didn't work out as planned, it opened the door for discouragement. Finally, discouragement comes when you think you're all alone. Have you ever been in a place where you think that you're the only one that's doing work or doing the right thing? Now see, that's a challenge, that's one of the things that the enemy tries to do—to isolate you in your thinking and have you to think you are the only one. This way he begins to pick apart your belief system and how you think. When the truth is that you're really never alone. God has people praying for you, even if it is on the other side of the world. They may not know your name or what is happening in your life, but God leads them to the intercede, supplicate and pray the perfect will for your life.

Several years ago, there was a movie made entitled "The Wizard of Oz"; you may also recall an adaptation of the film entitled, 'The Wiz'. There was a major character in the film called the Cowardly Lion. Now, when you think about it, the label of "cowardly lion" is an oxymoron and really doesn't go together. Lions in the animal kingdom are typically known as the "King of the Beasts". If there were cowardly lions in the jungle, they wouldn't last long and would quickly be done away with by other animals. I'd like to look at a few characteristics of the Cowardly Lion from the Wizard of Oz. What I'm endeavoring to do is to get you to think and have a better understanding of Biblical courage and boldness. So, I'm going to look at the opposite of this topic to emphasize what's being taught on or talked about. A couple of my spiritual mentors would use this same teaching method from time-to-time.

One of the characteristics of the Cowardly Lion was his habit of saying, "I'll think about it" rather than giving a decisive 'Yes' or 'No'. Where in contrast, Scripture tells us in Matthew 5:37; *'Let your Yes be simply Yes, and you're*

No be simply No; anything more than that comes from the evil one' (Amplified). In other words, you need to be decisive. But, when you lack courage you often are indecisive. It's amazing that people will leave a decision open for discussion although they know the answer, even in relation to sin and disobedience. There are certain suggestions that when they come to you, the answer should be an immediate NO. As a result of a lack of courage and confidence, you may leave the suggestion open for thought. Why think about it when you really should shut the door to it and just say 'NO'? Then some people over think things or analyze them to the point of it becoming a hindrance. Clearly, you should take time to think before you do things, but when you overthink you often end up doing nothing.

Another characteristic of the Cowardly Lion is that he always avoided conflict. He would shy away from anything that was challenging, even when it was necessary for the good. I know it's uncomfortable when a conflict or confrontation takes place, but there are times when you should stand your ground. A line in the sand must be drawn, and you say, "What's RIGHT is RIGHT! I'm going to stand up for what is RIGHT, and I'm not going to move away from it. If you don't agree with RIGHT, then we're going to be at odds." The intent is not to be malicious, dogmatic or to hurt anyone's feelings, but you should take a stand for some things and stand against others. If you always shy away from conflicts, you will never experience any victories.

Next, the Cowardly Lion was never willing to make any hard decisions. It takes confidence to make any difficult decision in your life. Those hard decisions are when you know you're not going to please everybody. One of my spiritual mentors used to say that one of the greatest miracles in Scripture was in Acts Chapter 6 when they appointed deacons. The Bible says that the decision pleased the whole *multitude*. He put that alongside Lazarus being raised from the dead since everybody was pleased with the decision. It's going to take some confidence to make decisions that some people are just not going to like. You'll have to have some confidence that you're making the right decision at the right time, regardless of what people think. There are times when you must make hard decisions about parenting, relationships, life and at work.

The fourth characteristic of the Cowardly Lion is that he pretended that everything was fine even though it was not. Sometimes, one may think that there will be lasting scar by which everyone will relate to us if it is exposed that help is needed. Some think that they will be knocked off their spiritual pedestal if they allow anybody to know they need help. There are times when it takes confidence to ask for help, rather than just to pretend it's okay. When you pretend you are operating on a falsehood and that is unstable. It takes confidence to admit that not everything is going the way it needs to go. It takes confidence to ask questions in that others may assume things are wrong. It doesn't change who you are; it only makes you better—the

Bible says, "iron sharpens iron". How does iron sharpen iron or how can a sister or brother sharpen another sister or brother? It happens when You let them know what's really going on and embrace their help.

The next characteristic is that the Cowardly Lion "cut out" on the team when situations became too difficult for him to handle. He lacked confidence and courage and ran away when times were tough, even when others were depending on him. Although I've not been in the military, I understand there are some military tactics and strategies that cause a soldier to depend on others. One person may have one direction of protection, and someone else might have another. All areas are to be protected unless one person abandons or walks away on the others--leaving the entire group completely vulnerable. It takes courage to stand firm, to remain, to fight and hang in there especially when others are depending on you and your part. A lack of courage, boldness, and confidence doesn't foster concern about whether others are dependent upon you because the main goal is to remove yourself from the fight; you simply want to get out of there! So, the cowardly person will say "Let them be vulnerable, I don't care at this point." The whole idea is self-preservation. When you run away from difficulties or challenging issues and refuse to back up team members, you are attempting to save yourself. This is a true sign of a lack of confidence.

Finally, the last characteristic of the Cowardly Lion is that he gave in to criticism, even when it was unfounded. Jesus, speaking to the disciples said in Mark 10, verses 27-30; *"But Jesus looked at them and said, "With men, it is impossible, but not with God; for with God all things are possible." (28) Then Peter began to say to Him, "See, we have left all and followed you." (29) So Jesus answered and said, "Assuredly, I say to you, there is no one who has left house or brothers or sisters or father or mother or wife or children or lands, for My sake and the gospel's, (30) who shall not receive a hundredfold now in this time—houses and brothers and sisters and mothers and children and lands, with persecutions -and in the age to come, eternal life."* Notice, Jesus ends by saying,"…with persecutions. "Understand, if you are going to do anything for God, people will criticize you, they will talk about you, up one side and down the other. However, if you're confident in who you are, confident in what you know you should be doing and confident in the Word of God, you'll say, "No matter what they say, I'm still going to do what God has told me to do." This should fuel your passion for doing what God has instructed you to do. Confidence overcomes criticism. Now that's something to talk about!

But Pastor, what about "constructive criticism"? Is there such a thing? Yes. There are those that want to facilitate Godly change in your life, by giving constructive criticism. The intent is not to undermine, condemn or pass judgment on you, but to provide insight and wisdom that will bless your life. And so, confidence would say, "Bless God let me make the change and move forward to the next level." But the lack of confidence will cause you to cower and 'run for cover'. When the enemy knows that you're operating in fear, he puts on a full attack. However, when you're able to stand flatfooted in the faith of God, believe in and stand on the Word of God, what comes out of your mouth is the Word of God. The enemy doesn't really understand if it's you or if it's the Lord Jesus Christ because you sound the same, you act the same and you look the same. The Bible says we've got to fight the good fight of faith. Everything is not going to come easy. Once you realize this, you won't wait around for something to be handed to you on a silver platter. Instead, you will step out and go after it.

Too many people are sitting back waiting for things, and amid their waiting, they become discouraged when what they're waiting for doesn't manifest. Being discouraged causes you to give up in the process and remove yourself from it. This automatically short-circuits what your belief in God. Don't be discouraged. Remember, Deuteronomy 31:6 encourages you to be strong and of a good courage.

Jesus provided some insight when he declared in Matthew 11:12, *"And from the days of John the Baptist until now the kingdom of heaven suffers violence, and the violent take it by force."* The Kingdom of God is always being assaulted. The devil hasn't rested one day from coming against the Kingdom. This scripture tells us that nothing will prevail against the Church of the living God. The Body of Christ wins. Although you win, it doesn't prevent Satan from attacking the Kingdom. But, you have everything you need to not only overcome Satan's attacks but to live in victory over the attacks! Hallelujah!

In Acts 4, both Peter and John taught the people of Jerusalem, in the name of the Lord Jesus Christ. Scripture tells us they were arrested, beaten and told not preach in that name any longer. The religious leaders and chief priests objected to their teaching and the many works that were accomplished. The leaders put Peter and John on trial insistently inquiring as to what power or authority did they teach and perform benevolent acts in their province. In Acts 4:23, the Bible states, *"And being let go, they went to their own companions and reported all that the chief priests and elders had said to them."* When Peter and John went to their own company and reported all that the chief priest and elders said to them, they lifted up their voice to God, with one accord and said in verses 24 and 25, *"So when they heard that, they raised their voice to God with one accord and said: "Lord, You are God, who made heaven and earth and the sea, and all that is in them, (25) who by the mouth of Your servant David have said: 'Why did the nations rage, And the people plot vain things?* Now, look at Verse 29, *"Now, Lord, look on their threats, and grant to your servants that with all boldness they may speak your word,"* Peter and John were arrested, beaten, and told by the leaders in the city, "Do not preach in the name Jesus any longer." Instead of packing up their bags and leaving, Peter and John went to their own companies, told them what was said, and they all began to pray and ask God to grant unto them boldness to speak the Word. What did this mean? Peter and John would go back to the very place they were threatened and beaten and preach the same Word, but preaching it with the *boldness* of God on them. They had more confidence in God than they had in the people who arrested them. Verse 31 says, *"And when they had prayed, the place where they were assembled together was shaken; and they were all filled with the Holy Spirit, and they spoke the word of God with boldness."* In other words, they got right back up, went right back into the city, where they were told not to go, and they preached the Word with *boldness*. As a result, Holy Spirit came in the midst and the entire place was shaken. These men were operating with and in boldness.

Encouraged to Pursue, Overtake and Recover All

The Bible describes David as a man after God's own heart. I believe he was a man after God's own heart primarily because he was quick to repent. David wasn't perfect, but when David realized he did something wrong, he would repent. David would get right back in the presence of God. He fixed whatever he could fix, and he just believed God that he could be right despite his mistakes.

The second reason why I believe that he was a man after God's own heart, is that David didn't back down from a challenge. As a young boy, he killed both a bear and a lion while attending sheep all alone on the backside of a mountain. As a young man, David found out that Goliath, the Philistine giant, defied the armies of the living God and there was a reward to the man that killed him. David told Saul, "Let me go out there and fight him. Just let me go. I don't need your armor. Just let me go out and fight this Philistine." David didn't back down. He went out before Goliath and said, *"You come to me with a sword, with a spear, and with a javelin. But I come to you in the name of the Lord of hosts, the God of the armies of Israel, whom you have defied. (46) This day the Lord will deliver you into my hand, and I will strike you and take your head from you. And this day I will give the carcasses of the camp of the Philistines to the birds of the air and the wild beasts of the earth, that all the earth may know that there is a God in Israel."* (1 Samuel 17:45-46) David defeated Goliath as both armies looked on in amazement. David had courage and confidence in his God. I believe this really touches the heart of God, like faith does.

Faith requires courage, and it requires strength. Instead of believing what the circumstances say, you should stand firm and say, "I'm not concerned about how I feel, or how it looks. I believe the Word of God." That takes

> *You must believe the Word of God when circumstances say everything contrary to what the Word of God says.*

courage. When you're in faith, you can't be weak. The expected harvest may not manifest right away; it may take a bit more effort. You may have to believe God for more than three, four or five days. You should have the same kind of tenacity after three years that you had after three minutes. It takes courage and confidence in God.

In First Samuel 22, the Bible tells us of David's departure to the cave Adullam and how his family and those in his father's house sought after him in the cave. Every one of them that was in distress, or in debt or discontented found David and gathered themselves with him. David became the captain of about four hundred men. David ministered to these men and developed them into mighty men of valor. They were no longer in debt, discontented or distressed. These men were now men of war. They now had some possessions, and things were working on their behalf.

Over in Chapter 30 of First Samuel, it goes on to say that an event took place in the lives of David and these men. The story begins in verse one, *"Now it happened, when David and his men came to Ziklag, on the third day, that the Amalekites had invaded the South and Ziklag, attacked Ziklag and burned it with fire, (2) and had taken captive the women and those who were there, from small to great; they did not kill anyone, but carried them away and went their way."* When David and his mighty men were at war, there was a company of Amalekites that came in and destroyed their city and took their wives and families. Verse 3 goes on to say, *"David and his men came to the city, and there it was, burned with fire; and their wives, their sons, and their daughters had been taken captive."*

Remember, the men of valor were no longer in distress, debt or discontented. However, David and his men cried out and wept, until they couldn't weep anymore. The four hundred men spoke of stoning David because all were grieving for their sons and daughters and this caused David to be greatly distressed. The very same men that sought out David because they were distressed, in debt and discontent and were then developed into mighty men of valor wanted to kill the very man that helped them. Even at that moment, David encouraged himself in the Lord his God. He couldn't get encouragement from anyone around him, so David chose to encourage himself in the Lord. You should understand that sometimes there may not be people around us willing to encourage us, so you must get to a place where you can encourage yourself.

David realized he could not get a victory in the state of being distressed. He had a choice; either stay distressed and be defeated or encourage himself. He chose to encourage himself. No one else was there. They were on the other side plotting to stone him. Who was going to encourage him beside himself? David encouraged himself in the Lord and inquired of the Lord whether he should pursue his enemies. God answered by saying, "Pursue, for you shall surely overtake *them* and without fail to *recover all."* Notice the difference in David after he encouraged himself. He was weeping when he was distressed, but after he encouraged himself in the Lord, he said, "Should I get up and go after them?" In other words, courage and boldness were stirred up on the inside of David so much so that he sought God and asked, "God should I go get them?" David got his men together and began to pursue them, and when they fell upon the camp, they found the company celebrating the victory that they had gotten, from the spoils from the land of the Philistines and the land of Judah. But, David and his men, from twilight, of the previous day, to the evening of the next day, fought to take back what had been stolen from them.

Sometimes, when you want back what has been stolen from you, you want it easy. Often you don't want to have to fight for it. Look at the example of David; he fought for a whole day and a half. You must understand what's needed when you commit to believing God. No matter what may come your way; come high water, low water or no water at all, you are going to believe God, step out and fight. You're going to pursue, overtake and *recover all!*

Righteousness is Armor in the Midst of Battles

No matter what, it is your responsibility to release your faith and fight the good fight of faith. How do you fight the good fight of faith? It is with the Armor of God. Second Corinthians 6:7 says that *"we have or we overcome by the armor of righteousness."* So, when you are the righteousness of God, you stand for righteousness and that righteousness will be a shield for you. Righteousness will be armor for you in the midst of the battle. Paul, in Ephesians 6:10-13, said to believers, *"Finally, my brethren, be strong in the Lord and the power of His might. (11) Put on the whole armor of God that you may be able to stand against the wiles of the devil. (12) For we do not wrestle against flesh and blood, but against principalities, against powers, against the rulers of the darkness of this age, against spiritual hosts of wickedness in the heavenly places. (13) Therefore take up the whole armor of God that you may be able to withstand in the evil day, and having done all, to stand."* Who uses armor? Those who are ready to fight.

Satan only offers suggestions and opportunities that you can choose to participate in or resist. He cannot make you do a single thing, as a child of God. No matter how much he tries, he cannot! However, if you open the door, he will come in. He'll offer you a suggestion, and if you take that suggestion, you'll bring about the consequences on yourself. He doesn't do it; you do it to yourself. Let me give you an example. Maybe Satan sends a thought to your mind that you're not going to make it, that you're about to go under, that you're going to lose everything. When that thought comes to your mind, and you say, "I'm not going to make it." The devil isn't talking, you are. What did you just do? You just condemned yourself. You gave voice to it. People will say, "Well, the devil did it." No, the devil didn't do anything but offer you a suggestion and an opportunity, and you took it.

Let me be clear; the fight is never with people, so you're wasting your time fighting individuals. Whether it's a foe or someone who is supposed to be a brother, when you're fighting against people, you're wasting your time. You're wasting your time because the person is not the issue. It's the influence of the person. The weapons that Paul goes on to mention in Ephesians chapter 6 are all spiritual. Each piece designed to protect us as we're on the offensive. The armor is not designed for us to run and hide. Truth, the Gospel of peace, righteousness, faith, salvation, and the Word of God, these are ALL spiritual. No natural weapons, because natural weapons aren't needed for a spiritual battle. You're not fighting against flesh, but against the influence of the attack. You already have the victory, and you should endeavor to maintain that victory.

Everything that God has promised you, you have a right to. The only one that's trying to keep it from you is the enemy himself, and he's already defeated. So, take out your weapons, the Armor of God, and pursue, overtake and ***recover all!***

Shout out loud, "I WILL PURSUE, OVERTAKE AND RECOVER ALL BECAUSE I AM THE RIGHTEOUSNESS OF GOD IN CHRIST JESUS!"

Chapter 9

Confidence: God's Nature and Your Potential

*"By fearful and glorious things [that terrify the wicked but
make the godly sing praises] do you answer us in
righteousness (rightness and justice), O God of our
salvation, You who are the confidence and hope of all the
ends of the earth and of those far off on the seas;"*
Psalm 65:5 Amplified Bible

Courage is what you need to do what's right and to step
out when others say that you can't do it. Courage is the
mental and moral strength to withstand danger, fear or
difficulty. It is the ability to stand on the Word, even though
you may be tempted with fear or worry. No matter what it
looks like, how it feels, what's going on around you, what
people are saying, you make an unwavering decision, a
choice, to stay on the Word of God. Courage enables you to
look in the face of challenges and not be moved.

In the book of Genesis, it is revealed that man was made in
the image and likeness of God. God gave man dominion
and blessed him to be able to prosper. From this revelation,
it's important to understand that God used Himself as the
prototype to create you and I. God, Himself, is a three-part

being; He's Father, Son and Holy Spirit. Therefore, you and I are a three-part being; spirit, soul, and body. Through this creation process, God imparted to man His image. The word '*image*' literally means *nature* or *characteristics.*

So, when God created you, He put His nature in you--the very nature of God is on the inside of each of born again child of God. Remember Second Corinthians 5:17? It said that your old nature passed away because your spirit man was recreated and a new nature was imparted. That new nature resembles or is the essence of God's nature. Not only is His nature in you, but you've been given the characteristics of God. By nature, you have some things that your spiritual parent, God, has. There are things He has put in you when you are born again. By His Spirit, He endeavors those things to be seen and demonstrated through you. Your nature is to win and be victorious. It might look like you're losing, but the buzzer has not rung yet, keep fighting a good fight of faith. You are on an undefeated team, and the captain of that team is Almighty God, who has never lost and will never lose. You will come out on top. You must understand whose side you are on. Which side of the field will you choose to stand on; God's side, the undefeated team, or the other side, the defeated team? Friend, you have the potential for greatness on the inside of you. Your potential, as the child of God, has nothing to do with the achievements of your family and friends, but it has to do with how you become aware of and how you respond to what God has put on the inside of you.

INWARD: Understanding Your True Nature In Christ

Potential is what you are capable of doing, not what you have done. You can do more.

What are you capable of doing, but haven't done yet? What ability is lying dormant waiting to be released? What is the untapped might on the inside of you just laying dormant waiting for you to reach down and take hold of it? Another mentor of mine once said, "The richest place on earth is the cemeteries because that's where the greatest treasure of untapped potential can be found." How many people have died without tapping the real potential that's on the inside of them? They died average or below average. They took that potential to the grave because only they could deposit their potential in the earth. Fear, a lack of understanding and persecution can cause people not to tap into their potential. Persecution is really designed to push you to your destiny. Believers need to learn and understand the things of God because persecution will occur. Second Timothy 3:12 states, *"Yes, and all who desire to live godly in Christ Jesus will suffer persecution."* However, Philippians 4:13 teaches that you CAN do all things through Christ that strengthens you. At salvation, when you receive Christ, you also receive all the strength needed, at that moment, to do all things. Really, there's no reason why you are not fulfilling what God has called or assigned you to do. There's no reason why you shouldn't be receiving all that God has promised.

I'll illustrate potential by comparing and relating it to the horsepower of an automobile. As you may know, horsepower is the unit of measure for the power of a vehicle. Some vehicles have more horsepower than others. A V6 engine can have more than 200 horsepower. However, other vehicles have a horsepower of 425, while there are others with 600-horsepower or more. What am I saying? A 600-horsepower car can be rated to reach speeds close to 200 miles per hour; however, the roads in the United States are not designed for a person to drive that fast. It's designed for upwards to 70 miles per hour on the Interstate. Although a driver is unable to drive close to the vehicle's potential of 200 miles per hour in the United States, just knowing the vehicle has the ability causes them drive a little bit different. This knowledge of the vehicle's ability provides more confidence when the need arises to step out and pass an 18-wheeled tractor trailer on an incline. When it's time to get it done, it gets done. As soon as there's a tap on the accelerator, all cylinders start to work in unison making quick work of the pass. On the contrary, a driver of a small energy-efficient vehicle with 70 horsepower may think twice before attempting to pass the same semi-truck. What's the difference? The knowledge of the vehicle's ability determines how confident a driver is while driving. The same can be said about the believer that understands their true nature in Christ. Once you see what has been promised to the child of God, instead of being timid, you go after those things. You hit the "accelerator" and tap into the potential that's on the inside of you. It's going to take you around any challenge or obstacle right into your divine destiny. Why are some believers not tapping into this potential? What are the hindrances to stepping into or tapping into this potential? Sometimes it's simply the fact that no one has taught on this potential on the inside. Using the car illustration, to enjoy its capabilities you would need proper information on its specifications. The same is for you. If you do not have proper information regarding your true nature, how can you enjoy all that it provides?

Another hindrance is your last successful project. While this answer isn't one that you would connect with as being a hindrance because you would think that the success would propel you to the next success. But, I've come to find out that a lot of people 'camp out' or build memorials at the place of their last success. When someone experiences one success, they are so glad something finally worked in their favor that they are afraid to try anything else. Instead, they spend the rest of their life trying to protect the last success instead of stretching forward to achieve another one. Isaiah 43:18 states, *"Do not remember the former things, nor consider the things of old."* That's inclusive of *successes and failure. It continues, "Behold, I will do a new thing, now it shall spring forth; shall you not know it? I will even make a road in the wilderness and rivers in the desert."* You should praise God for all successes but not dwell on them. God always wants you to experience new things in Him. Make successes motivational tools, not memorials.

For example, Peter, James, and John went up on the mountain of transfiguration with Jesus and the glory of God manifested. Jesus was shining with the glory of God, and then they, the disciples, saw Elias and Moses. The disciples said, "Jesus, let us set up camp right here and let us make three tabernacles, let's set up our house right here. Let's just stay in the glory." Jesus did not allow this thought to prevail because there were more people to reach and minister to.

A third hindrance to releasing potential is failed attempts. As a result of past failures, many will begin to put limits on themselves, not based on what can be done but rather on what didn't happen. In these times, be careful not to compare yourself to others when you fail because comparison will almost always lead to discontentment. Everyone has a different situation and a different set of circumstances.

There's increase on the inside of you! There's enlargement on the inside of you! There's abundance on the inside of you! There's more on the inside of you. However, you must be willing to reach down and grab hold of it and take advantage of it. Successes or failures of others have no bearing on what you can or cannot do in life. You should use these experiences and learn what to do or what not to do. Don't allow it to limit you because there is great potential inside.

Being consumed with your deficits and problems while making excuses is the next hindrance. It's amazing how much time people spend talking about what they cannot do and very little time about what they can do, especially when the scripture says, "I can do all things." When this mindset is evident, it's easy to associate or fellowship with people who have the same 'can't do attitude". Instead get around those who have your answers, get rid of those with the "can't do" attitude and embrace a 'can do' attitude. God didn't put a line through your name because of the

> *The mistakes you make in life do not cancel out the plan of God for your life.*

mistakes you may have made in life. I don't think it excites God that you make mistakes, but I think it excites Him to have an opportunity to do something exceeding abundantly above and beyond what you can ask or think.

I'm reminded of the prodigal son, who was in the pigpen eating slop when he said, "Wait a minute, the servants in my father's house are eating even better than me. What am I doing hanging out with these pigs?" He got up, probably muddy, and went home. He said, "Father, just make me a servant. I'll serve you dinner every day, because I know I've made mistakes." His father replied, "What is wrong with you? You're not a servant in this house; you're a son." His father then turned to the hired servants and instructed them to clean up his son, kill the fattest cow, and plan a party because it's time to celebrate the return of his son. That's a picture of the heart of God! When you make a mistake. Go to God and acknowledge, "God, I've messed up. Forgive me." Your heavenly Father will receive you, clean you up and restore you. Praise God! The same inheritance that was ordained for you before the mistake, you still have after the mistake and through this loving restoration process.

The fifth hindrance to tapping into your potential is becoming stagnant in tradition. Just to be clear, tradition is not always something in the church, there are also traditions in a family. There can be a tradition in your life. What do I mean by that? Just doing the same thing repeatedly will lead to a mundane way of living which will cause you not to want to do anything different. Traditions and habits can cause your potential to be hindered as it causes you not to ask if there is a better way to do things.

Embrace the fact that you are full of potential. Not just any potential but divine potential, because of your true nature in Christ. Do not allow your potential to be hindered in any way because you are capable of doing so much more.

Shout out loud: "I HAVE THE POTENTIAL FOR GREATNESS ON THE INSIDE OF ME AND TODAY I CHOOSE TO TAP INTO IT! I AM THE RIGHTEOUSNESS OF GOD IN CHRIST JESUS!"

Chapter 10

Benefits of God's Righteousness: Part II

"Bless the Lord, O my soul; And all that is within me, bless His holy name! (2) bless the Lord, O my soul, And forget not all His benefits:"
Psalm 103:1-2

Another benefit of righteousness is: it causes you to reign in life. In other words, it causes you to be on top. Righteousness provides a position of authority because you are a Kingdom citizen. All Kingdom citizens have authority in the Kingdom of God, which is the basis to walk in authority in life.

Rejoice in scriptures such as:

"But thanks be to God, who gives us the victory through our Lord Jesus Christ." (1 Corinthians 15:57)

"Yet in all these things we are more than conquerors through Him who loved us." (Romans 8:37)

"And the Lord will make you the head and not the tail; you shall be above only, and not be beneath, if you heed

the commandments of the Lord your God, which I command you today, and are careful to observe them." (Deuteronomy 28:13)

This is your reality because of your position with God and your true nature in Christ. In Romans, Paul reveals that through the victory that Jesus achieved over sin, those who believe shall receive the gift of righteousness and shall reign in life. Unfortunately, terms like reign in life can be foreign to those in the body of Christ. Regardless, it is God's will for you to reign and have victory over everything that is contrary to your true nature in Christ. Friend, I know it may be a lot of discussion about how hard life can be. That's why you must understand who you are in Christ and the benefits that accompany that reality. You do not have to live like everyone else. God has provided a way living that you and I can enjoy and use to benefit others.

A Right to All the Promises of God

"For all the promises of God in Him are Yes, and in Him Amen, to the glory of God through us." (2 Corinthians 1:20) This scripture reveals that whatever God has already said yes to or whatever He has promised, you automatically get a "yes" when you ask Him for it. You may have heard someone say, sometimes God says no to your prayers. I found this out, if God is saying no to your prayers then you're praying for the wrong things. The Bible clearly shows us that He has already said, "Yes and Amen." That

means God has taken care of everything He needs to take care of. Now, it's your part to appropriate the promises of God by faith.

Healing is a 'Yes'. Prosperity is a 'Yes'. Peace is 'Yes'. Salvation is 'Yes'. You cannot find anywhere in history where anyone has come to God to be saved and God says, "You can't be saved." Nowhere! God has already said yes about it. The Bible states in James 4:2a-3, *"...you do not have because you do not ask. (3) You ask and do not receive, because you ask amiss, that you may spend it on your pleasures."* James is saying that you don't receive because you never ask or you ask for the wrong things or with the wrong motives. Really, the principles of prayer will work if you would simply cooperate with the principles of prayer. First John 5:14 confirms this by stating, *"Now this is the confidence that we have in Him, that if we ask anything according to His will, He hears us."* That means anything you find in God's Word that He has already appropriated, is yours when you ask Him for it, and He will hear the request. Friend, God hears you when you pray His Word. Continuing with verse 15, *"And if we know that He hears us, whatever we ask, we know that we have the petitions that we have asked of Him."* Some may tell you that God will not give you some things that you want. On the contrary, if you ask according to what He has promised, you will receive. That doesn't mean that it will manifest immediately, but if you continue to be in faith and hold fast to your confidence, all these things shall be added unto you. Just because the answer doesn't manifest the same day, it doesn't mean "No." It means you're still in the process. The Bible encourages you in Galatians, *"And let us not grow weary while doing good, for in due season we shall reap if we do not lose heart."* When you see it promised in the Word of God, be convinced and be confident. In layman's terms, face every day and say, "Bless God! He promised this to me, and I will not be denied!"

Romans 8:17 begins with, *"And if children..."* Using the word "children" denotes that it is referring to one that is born again. Not everyone is a child of God. However, everyone is a creation of God. You become a child of God when you receive salvation. It continues, *"...then heirs— heirs of God and joint heirs with Christ, if indeed we suffer from Him, that we may also be glorified together."* The Amplified Bible says it this way, *"And if we are [His] children, then we are [His] heirs also."*

As a child of God, He has made you an heir which means that you have joint ownership of the things of God. You are also joint heirs with Jesus Christ meaning you have equal right and access to everything Jesus possesses. The Amplified Bible puts it this way, *"We share in His inheritance."* God gave

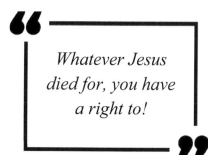

Whatever Jesus died for, you have a right to!

everything to Jesus, and Jesus gave everything to you. You are now a partaker of that inheritance since you are an heir with God. *Heir* means an inheritor; the beneficiary or a recipient. So, everything that God has, you have a right to. Guess what? Satan can't deny you. Other people can't deny you. The economy can't deny you. Nothing can deny you because you have a right to it. Choose to stand until it manifests.

Doing Business in the Kingdom of God

Again, when you are born again, you are translated out of darkness into the Kingdom of His dear son. Therefore, you are in the Kingdom of God. You belong to a different society. That's why it is important to note the instruction found in Romans 12:2 to not to be conformed to this world. By conforming to this world, you are inviting resistance against the Kingdom of God in which you reside. The Kingdom of God's principles is not the same as the world's principles. Some people live defeated, even though they are Kingdom citizens because they don't understand Kingdom laws and Kingdom principles. They are trying to live as Kingdom citizens by worldly laws and worldly principles which will not work. It short-circuits the benefits of righteousness. So, if you're in the Kingdom, you must live by Kingdom laws. For example, in the United States, there are certain laws that may not be the same or work the same in other countries. If you decided to move to another country, you wouldn't be able to take the law book for the

United States and think you can live there based on those laws. You would be subject to the laws that are in your new country of residence and should you unknowingly break the law there, your defense can't be "I'm from the United States, and it was not unlawful there." The same thing is true in the Kingdom of God. You must not be conformed to the world but conformed to the Kingdom. No longer can the excuse, "those in the world are doing it," be given. You have a new set of laws and principles to live by.

Matthew 6:33 states, *"But seek first the kingdom of God and His righteousness, and all these things shall be added to you."* Let me first clarify what is meant by the Kingdom of God. For years, this term has been misunderstood and misrepresented. The *Kingdom of God* is defined as the 1) system of God; 2) order of God; 3) realm of God and 4) the rule of God. It's God's way of doing things. Consequently, the statement 'His righteousness' is God's way of doing and being right. Once you become the righteousness of God, you need to cooperate with this specific principle.

Righteousness gives you the opportunity to work Kingdom laws and Kingdom principles. Righteousness then, allows you to operate Kingdom principles and laws and those principles and laws will work for you. You may wonder; why does God bless His family? It's Kingdom law. It's the way the Kingdom operates, and you are a partaker because of your righteousness. Kingdom principles and laws work so well that the world has realized the benefits associated with these principles and they've extracted and operated in them. Many have become successful by using many of the principles God intended for His family. While there may not be mention of scripture from the world, when they're teaching these principles in books and seminars, its Kingdom principles none the same. If the world can get results from operating in Kingdom principles, how much more should the family of God be getting greater results.

My point is: righteousness gives you the right to work these principles. All legitimate businesses are required to have a license to do business, and there are government mandated codes of regulations outlining what they can and cannot do. In the Kingdom of God, your license to do business is your righteousness, and the Word of God is the code of ethics and defines how you are going to conduct business. The Word serves as the directive in which you find out what you have a right to. The currency needed to take advantage of these rights is obedience and faith. Putting this all together concludes that you can do business in the Kingdom and get accelerated results.

Shout out loud, "I AM THE RIGHTEOUSNESS OF GOD IN CHRIST JESUS!"

Chapter 11

Righteousness: A Mode of Conduct

"I call heaven and earth as witnesses today against you, that I have set before you life and death, blessing and cursing; therefore choose life, that both you and your descendants may live;"
Deuteronomy 30:19

In previous chapters, I've discussed who you are in Christ and that your true nature is righteousness. Additionally, scripture reveals not only should righteousness be your nature, but righteousness should also be your mode of conduct. So, because of being righteous, you also do righteousness.

Remember that in the first several chapters, I identified that you don't do things to become righteous; you do things because you are righteous. You pray because you are righteous. You serve because you are righteous. So then, your works have nothing to do with your true nature in Christ, the righteousness of God. Your nature defines who you are more than what you do. Righteousness has everything to do with who God has made you because of receiving Jesus as Lord and Savior. However, now that you've been made righteous, you now need to participate in righteousness. If righteousness is your nature, then what should your actions represent? It should represent your nature, which is RIGHTEOUSNESS!

You may know people that may be challenged with telling the truth. Their nature is always to lie. And so, people refer to them as liars. Why? It's because their actions represent their nature. Likewise, if you are righteous, then your actions should speak of that nature. People can become confused when you say one thing, and they see something else. They step back and think to themselves, "Wait a minute, I hear what they're saying, but I'm also seeing what they're doing. What I'm seeing doesn't look like what they're saying." You think you're fooling others, but really, you are only fooling yourself.

God's righteousness, your true nature is right. With that being the case, you should be producing right. If righteous is who you are, then righteousness should be what you do. I believe there is a time coming where there will be a clear delineation of who is in the world, and who is of God. The line will no longer be skewed.

There are three types of beliefs that people operate by when talking about a mode of conduct. There is a reason why people believe the way they believe and their actions are in direct correlation to the way they believe. In fact, to change a person's actions, would require that person to change the way they think, which they will ultimately change the way they believe.

The first belief is that people operate their lives with the belief that God is in control of everything. "Well, Dr. Frye, isn't He?" Yes, God is omnipotent and all powerful. Yes, He's omniscient and all-knowing. Yes, He's omnipresent and all present. God can do whatever He decides to do whenever He decides to do it. But God has given His Word, and God has chosen to submit Himself to His Own Word. God will not do anything outside of His Word, so God is not in control of everything. I'll prove this with a few illustrations. If God were in control of everything, everyone would be saved. There would be no unsaved person on the face of this earth. Why? Because it's God's will that all men be saved. If God were in control of everything, every child of God would love one another. That's if God were in control. My third example is, if God were in control, no one would rob God of the tithe. Just by these three points, we know that God is not in control of everything. This may come as a surprise, but it's the truth.

The second type of belief that people operate by is that the Satan is in control of everything. I'm sure you've heard people say, "The devil did it." You may have heard someone say "Ain't anything but the devil. The devil has been chasing me." I realize the grammar is bad, but it's a common phrase for those who don't know better. People who live in this arena live in fear because fear comes from the devil, which comes from darkness. You should know the devil is not in control because if he were, no one would be saved. If he were in control, he would stop everybody from coming to the Lord. If he were in control, there would be no one walking in love with anyone. There would be no one honoring God with their giving. He wouldn't allow any of us to give to God, to help further the gospel on this earth. So, he is not in control of everything. Understand that decisions and choices create circumstances and a certain quality of life. Since you've chosen to get saved and chosen to learn the Word of God, you've then chosen to have a better quality of life. God didn't make you do it. The devil didn't make you do it. You chose it.

Since the Garden of Eden, there has been a game played of "who gets the blame, " and it's going to continue until a new heaven and new earth come. It's the easy way out of consequences. The remarkable thing about choices is that they are so powerful that God must honor all of them. He must honor your choices and all

> *You can have a better quality of life if the choices you make were better.*

your decisions because He has given you a free choice; a will of your own. Although people may make foolish choices, God doesn't come down and erase them. He will acknowledge and honor the choice, and help you walk through the consequences. God endeavors to speak, encourage and instruct before a choice is made. In a still small voice, He'll say, "Don't do that or go for it." "That's the wrong move or way to go." "Not now or perfect timing." There are times when you move out on your own and make the wrong choice. If that is the case, God must honor that. However, God is so good that as soon as you make the wrong decision, He starts speaking, encouraging and instructing you on how to overcome the wrong choice and make better choices in the future.

Let's look at Deuteronomy 30:19 which says, *"I call heaven and earth as witnesses today against you, that I have set before you life and death, blessing and cursing; therefore choose life, that both you and your descendants may live;"* He has given you the test and the answer. Why should you choose life? It's so that you and your seed may live. It's talking about a quality of life. Your quality of life is affected by your choices you make in life. Friend choose life!

In Matthew 16, Peter received the revelation that Jesus was the Christ, the Son of the living God; the revelation that Jesus would build His church upon. And then in Verse 19, the Bible states, *"And I will give you the keys of the kingdom of heaven, and whatever you bind on earth will be bound in heaven, and whatever you loose on earth will be loosed in heaven."* The choice is made on earth, and then heaven backs up the choice. What I'm saying is God will honor the choices you make, and the choices you make will affect the quality of life that you live. Never forget, life is choice driven!

Conduct is a standard of personal behavior based on principles. All live based on a standard that has been set. Some have a set of higher standards for themselves than others. There are some things that some won't do, but there are some things others will do. This is all based on the standard that has been set to govern life. Over the course of your life, you've been given information; some right and some wrong. As such, there are people, including myself, that had a standard of behavior based on that wrong information which caused things in life to be out of order. When life is based on wrong information, it is important to recognize it's wrong and make a choice to change. That's where "the rubber meets the road." Because, you can know to do better, but until you choose to, you will not live better. I don't think it's wise to know that you're doing something wrong and then choose to continue to do it but expect different results. Somebody defined the word insanity as doing this very thing; doing the same thing but expecting different results.

Your standard of living is tied to the information that you've received over time. There have been relatives, friends, teachers, etc. that had a collaborative effort in pouring into your life. Some people poured good things and others not so good. Based on the authority or influence that you gave them determined how much you would act on the information they shared with you. Some people become successful in life, and they tie their success to someone in their past like an elementary school teacher, who may have spoken some things into their life or maybe a little league or high school football or basketball coach. All throughout life, people are pouring into your life, giving information and imparting what they know into your life. At some point, your life will line up with all the information that has been received over your lifetime. Now that you understand your true nature in Christ, you can use the Word of God to sift out what is wrong and let what is right remain.

Each need to ask these questions, "What standard have I set for my life?" "Is my standard set high or is it set on middle ground?" "Do I have a low standard in my life?" Standards can be examined by what you will allow and what behaviors you participate in. Sometimes, you may not do a certain thing, but allowing it will be as if you're condoning the practice. Although you are not participating in the activity, by not saying something, you are communicating with others that it's alright. You must have a standard which should be high. The best option is to make your standard the Word of God. If I can be candid about it, there are only two ways that you can lay hold of things in life: 1) your way or 2) God's way. It can be achieved by your way of doing things or simply by obeying God.

Often, when there is talk about placing standards on people's lives, people begin to make up excuses as to why they can't do what the Word of God is calling for. It's as if their situation causes them to act or behave this way. No, situations shouldn't dictate your behavior; your choices should be based on the standards you have set.

You may hear people say, "They **made** me so mad." When they examine it properly, they will understand that an opportunity to be angry was presented and a choice was made to respond in anger. It's the same in your case. Someone can present you an opportunity to be angry, but you do not have to respond the same way others do. You can choose to respond differently. You can have peace with it all. It's possible. You can choose to live life carefree. It doesn't matter what's going on around you. Once the decision is made, people can't steal your joy, you've set that standard for your life, then it doesn't matter what's going on, nobody is going to steal your joy!

Let's focus on excuses for a minute or two. What are excuses? An excuse is simply a crutch for the uncommitted. I think the number one excuse people make for not serving God, is that they think living for God is too hard which is so far from the truth. People make things harder than they need to be. Really, it just takes discipline, with some commitment, understanding, and information to live the way God wants you to live. If it were impossible to do, he would never require it.

Sometimes, when you're learning something new or entering to a class for the first time, the information is so unfamiliar that it's difficult to grasp. It's difficult, but it's not impossible because people had come before you and learned. People, who are in class with you, are learning it, and people will come after you and learn it. So, it's not impossible. It may be challenging, but if you do what you need to do; if you show up for class, pay attention, listen, study and do your homework, the result should be that you've learned something. So, what was challenging at first now becomes easier basically because you did your part. That's the same thing with the Word of God. You must have a level of commitment to do the Word of God. The more you do the Word, the easier it will become to obey the Word and harder to disobey the Word.

I'm talking about righteousness being a mode of conduct. God has called you to righteousness and true holiness. So, if God has called you to that, then you're to do that. Proverbs 13:15 KJV states, *"Good understanding giveth favor: but the way of the transgressor is hard."* This scripture doesn't say the way of the righteous, but the way of the transgressor. Transgressor means someone who knows what to do but chooses to go against what they know. Life is hard trying to do things against what you know to do. Understand that a life of disobedience to God will end up hard and will wear on you. It will cause you to age faster, be worn out in your body and hinder you from receiving the best of God. Friend, it's easy to obey God because you've been created to obey God. You've been given the grace and Holy Spirit, to help you obey God. Really, that excuse for it being too hard to serve God is really no excuse at all.

Another excuse is "I can't. I just simply can't." Philippians 4:13 states, *"I can do all things through Christ which strengthens me."* Don't ever think you're doing anything alone. God is always doing it with you, not for you. Therefore, there's nothing in life that you can't do, since God is always with you. Understand that to enjoy the benefit of everything you're entitled to as a righteous child of God, you must choose to live your life according to God's order established by His Word. Remember Matthew 6:33, instructs to seek first the Kingdom of God and His righteousness. You found out earlier that the Kingdom of God is God's government, it's God's realm, it's God's system on earth and His righteousness is His way of doing things and being right. Therefore, not only are you seeking His system, His order, His government, but you are also seeking His way of being right. To live according to God's order, you must put aside your desires and your way of doing things. This will allow you to tap into what God has designed for you to enjoy.

Look at Acts 10:34. I want you to see something here that I think is incredible. It states, *"Then Peter opened his mouth and said: "In truth, I perceive that God shows no partiality. But in every nation whoever fears Him and works righteousness is accepted by Him."* First, Peter reveals that God shows no partiality. Friend, God loves all the same. Glory to God! I'm His favorite. You're His favorite. All of God's children are His favorites. Amen! Verse 35 continues, *"But in every nation whoever fears*

Him and works righteousness is accepted by Him." Glory to God!!! The Amplified Bible says it this way, *"But in every nation, he who venerates and has a reverential fear for God, treating Him with worshipful obedience and living uprightly, is acceptable to Him and sure of being received and welcomed [by Him]."* This passage of scripture reveals that God leans towards those who do righteousness. Certainly, He respects all the same, but then, when it comes to people working righteousness, it really gets God's attention. God is not showing favoritism; it's just that He has the propensity to move towards those who are doing righteousness more than others. Remember, anybody who is a child of God can choose to do righteousness. Let that minister to you. When you choose to do righteousness, you know the Lord is receiving you. Glory to God!

First John 2:28 states, *"And now, little children, abide in Him, that when[a] He appears, we may have confidence and not be ashamed before Him at His coming."* Jesus is coming for the Church, and the Church should be ready for His coming. He said that He's going to come as a thief in the night. He didn't say a specific year, month or day. You must get it in your hearts that no matter when He comes you will be ready for His coming and not be ashamed. Verse 29, Amplified Bible, states, *"If you know(perceive and are sure) that He[Christ] is[absolutely] righteous[conforming to the Father's will in purpose, thought, and action], you may also know (be sure) that everyone who does righteously [and is therefore in like manner conformed to the divine will] is born (begotten) of Him [God]."* The truth is this, if you are of Him, if you are in Him, you are expected and meant to behave like Him. Righteousness is behavior that's representative of your true nature in Christ. So, since you are righteous, living righteous is what you do!

Shout out loud, "I AM THE RIGHTEOUSNESS OF GOD THEREFORE I CHOOSE TO DO RIGHTEOUSNESS!"

Chapter 12

CHOICES IN CONDUCT:
Honoring God By Hitting The Mark

*"But God be thanked that though you were slaves of sin,
yet you obeyed from the heart that form of doctrine to
which you were delivered. (18) And having been set free
from sin, you became slaves of righteousness."*
Romans 6:17-18

There is not much mention of sin coming from the pulpits throughout America, but it is something that needs to be dealt with. When I was growing up in my local church, sin was all I heard. However, no one ever told me how to overcome sin. They just told me that I was a sinner saved by grace and that I would never do anything right; I would always do wrong.

Over time, this kind of thinking develops into a sin consciousness that is, the thought that you'll never be right. So, I don't want to talk about sin at a level where you can't overcome it because when you are born again, you overcame sin. Amen! The Bible teaches that sin has no more power over you. That means it doesn't control you anymore. But, you can still choose to do it. For that reason, each should make the earnest choice not to participate in sin.

When one disobeys God, it reveals disrespect for Him and documents that there is a lack of fear or reverence. Your obedience is the proof that you have faith and trust completely in Him. With that said, I would like to deal with the different levels of disobeying of God to give you an understanding of how your behavior should be a representation of your true nature in Christ.

What is a sin? Sin is simply defined as missing the mark. If you've ever played darts, look at it as the bull's eye on the board. When a player hits the wall instead of the dart board, they not only missed the bull's eye but the entire dartboard. Clearly, they missed the mark. There was a goal or target in which the player was trying to hit, and because the throw was off, they simply missed the mark. And so, it's the same thing in life. There is a target that you should be aiming for that has been established by God. There are times where your actions fall short, or your actions fall outside of the mark, in which He has set for your life. As a result sin occurs. After the born-again experience, you should get out of the practice of sin. The habitual, purposeful acts of sin should begin to wane. However, because you are not perfect, you may fall into sin occasionally. There is a big difference between falling into sin and planning to sin. Every action is preceded by a thought. There's a thought first, which means you are aware of it.

When sin is not dealt with properly, it moves into transgression. *Transgression* is doing what's wrong even when you know it's wrong. Your will is being set to go along with the transgression. Transgression is action. Sin can occur in your thinking, yet transgression involves an action that causes you to go against the grain of what you know is right. The best place to catch disobedience is in the "sin" stage. This allows you to deal with it internally and make the necessary adjustments before you carry it out. However, as soon as you transgress, it shows you have thought about it, planned it and acted on it.

Repeated transgressions lead to a state of iniquity. Iniquity is the result of sin and transgression being practiced until it becomes habitual. Iniquities can become so strong that they can be transferred from generation to generation. The Bible speaks of God allowing the iniquities of the father to go down to the third and fourth generations. This means when sin and transgression are practiced to the place where it becomes habitual, it opens the door for the same iniquity to be handed down to the next generations.

There must be a choice to live according to the Word of God, so a new way of living is established for you and the next generation. Once you commit to this choice, it will quickly become a normal way of life. It takes the challenge out of endeavoring to obey God. God's Word should set the boundaries of your life. In those times when you may go outside the Word of God, you should realize that you are out of bounds and going against the things of God. It's up to you to repent and get back in the game. Repent means to turn and go the other way. Repentance has nothing to do with feeling sad, sorry or crying; it has to do with turning and going the other way. Choosing to obey God and having a conduct of righteousness or operating in righteousness demonstrates to the world your true nature in Christ.

Reasons Why to Operate in Righteousness

Operating in righteousness reveals the nature of God. Others get to see God in you. The day is here where people will really need to see genuine children of God operating in their true nature in Christ. Second Corinthians 5:20 declares that we are ambassadors for Christ. The position of an ambassador is to be a representative. An Ambassador is the highest diplomatic official sent from one country to another to carry out the orders and the assignment of the country from which they're sent. As an ambassador of Christ, you are the highest diplomatic official from Heaven. You are in the earth to carry out the orders of the Kingdom of God on behalf of God. You are in the world, but you are not of the world. You are on the earth, but not subject to the confines of it because you are supported by the unlimited source of Heaven. Obedience and a conduct of righteousness reveal God in the earth.

The second reason why you should do righteousness or have a conduct of righteousness is to remind Satan that he is already defeated. From time to time, Satan needs to be reminded that you don't have to succumb to darkness anymore and that he no longer has control of you. You now possess the light of God's Word and the revelation of your true nature in Christ. So, every time you choose to do right, every time you choose to obey God, Satan is reminded that he is not in control anymore. He's reminded that he doesn't control nor exercise any form of authority over your life. Every time you say "Yes" to God and "No" to him, he is reminded that he is a defeated foe.

The third reason you should do righteousness or have a conduct of righteousness is that the righteous are rewarded. Let's look at Psalm 84:11 which states, *"For the Lord God is a sun and shield; The Lord will give grace and glory; No good thing will He withhold from those who walk uprightly."* When you choose to walk uprightly, God will not hold any good thing from you. The Amplified Bible says it this way, *"For the Lord God is a Sun and Shield; the Lord bestows [present] grace and favor and [future] glory (honor, splendor, and heavenly bliss)! No good thing will he withhold from those who walk uprightly."* Walking uprightly is walking in righteousness. Choosing to walk in righteousness is a choice to have a conduct of righteousness. In other words, you should expect to be rewarded when you walk in righteousness. This is true even when dealing with natural parents. When children come home with good grades when they obey and do their chores and keep their room clean. parents are pleased to reward them. When they have bad attitudes or decide not to do anything they have been instructed, parents are less likely to reward them.

Ways to Function in the Conduct of Righteousness

There are three practical ways in which to function in this conduct of righteousness. While it's good to know about it, it also needs to be done. The blessings manifest by doing not by just knowing. Yes, it's good to know it because knowing provides us with the ability to do, but don't stop just at knowing. The book of James declares, "Be doers of the word, not hearers only."

The first way to walk in this conduct of righteousness is to learn self-control. First Thessalonians 4:1-4 states, *"Finally then, brethren, we urge and exhort in the Lord Jesus that you should abound more and more, just as you received from us how you ought to walk and to please God; for you know what commandments we gave you through the Lord Jesus. For this is the will of God, your sanctification: that you should abstain from sexual immorality; that each of you should know how to possess his own vessel in sanctification and honor,"* The Amplified translation tells us, *"That each one of you should know how to possess, control and manage his own body in consecration, purity, separated from things profane and honor."* Self-control equated to knowing how to possess your vessel/body. Let me put it this way, there's some information that you alone know about yourself and because of that, you ought to take that information and learn how to possess, control and manage your body/vessel. You are the only one that can control you. External things such as policies, procedures, and guidelines may be in place, but if you don't know how to control yourself, you'll still misbehave even though there are guidelines in place. Self-control is not based on external sources; it should be based on the knowledge you have gained through knowing the order in which God expects you to live. You are aware of the areas you are weak. Therefore, use that information to begin the process of fortifying your life with the principles and guidelines of the Word of God. Feeding the areas that are challenging you to keep it alive. Whatever you feed gets fat. It grows and stays alive. The only way to kill it is to starve it; cut it off from its life source.

The second way is to learn how to purge. Purge means to cleanse and cut off and is a beneficial activity in your life. On a consistent and regular basis, you need to purge people, places, and things. While this may sound severe, it's necessary because if you're not careful and your guard is let down, you may end up associating with the wrong people in the wrong places and doing the wrong things. A constant review of your life and making the proper adjustments will enable you to stay on track.

Purging in the plant kingdom causes something to grow more. Remember, Jesus, said in John 15:2, *"Every branch in me that does not bear fruit He takes away; and every branch that bears fruit He prunes, that it may bear more fruit.*" Let me just say, purging isn't fun; however, it is beneficial. Some things that you need to go through and do for your life might not be comfortable at the time, but it will benefit you overall. The way you cleanse your way is to take heed to the Word of God. Cleansing and changing your way should come through paying attention to and observing the Word. Awareness needs to take place and allow righteousness to be a light to you so that you don't act on the opportunity of sin. Hebrews 12:1 states, *"Therefore we also, since we are surrounded by so great a cloud of witnesses, let us lay aside every weight, and the sin which so easily ensnares us, and let us run with endurance the race that is set before us,"* I have run track on the collegiate level and I can relate to running with and without weights. Running without weights is much more conducive to putting you in a position to win. Romans 12:1 follows this thought by stating, *"I beseech you, therefore, brethren, by the mercies of God, that you present your bodies a living sacrifice, holy, acceptable to God, which is your reasonable service."* Presenting your body is an act of worship. By saying "No" to the flesh and "YES" to God, you are worshipping God even though you might not have your hands up or music might not be playing in the background. Choosing to uphold righteousness over the way of men and the ways of the flesh is an act of worshipping the Father.

Presenting your body to God means to choose to release personal desires and embrace God's will. How is that done? It's done by developing your mind to the point that your thinking shadows God's thinking. That is an agreement with God and true worship on one accord. As you're practically walking out your conduct of righteousness, you need to be in a continual process of possessing, keeping your body under control, under subjection, purging yourself of people, places and things that will come in and try to pull you off the track that God has laid out for your life.

> *Whatever God says "Yes" to you say "Yes" to. Whatever God says "No" to you say "No" to.*

Finally, you must learn how to present yourself as a living sacrifice. I love the way the Bible presents a living sacrifice as having choices. A dead sacrifice no longer has choices, but a living one does. You can choose to lay your life on the altar of God and say, "God, here I am. What you say yes to, I say yes to, what you say no to, I say no to. Here I am God!" Every morning is a good time to say, "Here am I God and I say yes to you!" and present your body as a living sacrifice. Then all of Heaven becomes available to you because you are the righteousness of God in Christ Jesus and therefore you do righteousness.

Shout out loud, "I AM THE RIGHTEOUSNESS OF GOD IN CHRIST JESUS!!"

Chapter 13

Trees of Righteousness

"To console those who mourn in Zion, To give them beauty for ashes, The oil of joy for mourning, The garment of praise for the spirit of heaviness; That they may be called trees of righteousness, The planting of the Lord, that He may be glorified."
Isaiah 61:3

Isaiah declares the children of God as "trees of righteousness." Think about that for a moment; trees of righteousness. Consider the structure and operation of a natural tree. Its core makeup is a trunk or stem, roots, and branches. The trunk of a tree provides strength and aids in carrying materials throughout different parts of the tree. It provides support to the branches and leaves as well.

The roots function so that nutrients and moisture are extracted from the soil and are provided to the entire tree. They then transport materials throughout the tree and secure it. The roots of a tree keep soil from eroding which maintains the stability of the tree. The entire root system is the foundation for the tree. The roots of most trees grow deep, spread out wide and, as they mature, can penetrate and upend ground. There are some trees, such as the Redwood, where the roots are not deep; however, they interweave with surrounding trees, thereby providing each other with strength and keeping each one secure and steady.

Branches on a tree bear buds or shoots, which usually produce leaves, needles or fruit. Leaves then capture energy from light, through a process known as photosynthesis, which then converts it to food which is needed by the tree to grow, develop and mature. This nourishment is critical to the life of the tree. This process is a great illustration of the spiritual life of a Believer. In John 15, Jesus instructs the disciples to abide in Him because a branch cannot bear the fruit of itself, apart from abiding in the vine (stem). Jesus declares that He is the vine (stem) and you and I are the branches and when properly abiding in Him will bear an abundance of fruit. In likeness to the roots of a tree, Jesus, through the Spirit of God, develops, sustains and strengthens you. He provides the very power you need to live a life within the boundary and principles of God's Word. That power is righteousness, and it's infused with your spirit. It not only provides every believer with the privilege of having fellowship with God, but it's a power and force that makes it possible for each believer to conform and be transformed to the very image of Jesus. Due to this power, your life should continually increase and elevate in and with God from one level to the next. Once one level is attained, continue to move on to the next and then another; seeing yourself carrying out scripture by going from glory to glory. *"Now the Lord is the Spirit, and where the Spirit of the Lord is, there is liberty (emancipation from bondage, freedom). (18) And all of us, as with unveiled face, [because we] continued to behold [in the Word of God] as in a mirror the glory of the Lord, are constantly being transfigured into His very own image in ever increasing splendor and from one degree of glory to another; [for this comes] from the Lord [Who is] the Spirit.* (2 Corinthians 3:17-18 AMP)

Righteousness then provides confidence and assurance in your ability to walk out the plan of God. God's righteousness is the heart, and it is to shape and influence the spirit of the child of God. So, just as the roots of a tree go deeper and spread, indicating its growth and maturation, having confidence in God and His way of doing and being right, empowers, energizes and strengthens you to do and be right, causing spiritual growth. Just as a natural tree receives energy from light, you too receive light; the illumination of God's Word. Holy Spirit imparts the power of God, which permeates your heart to develop and produce spiritual growth. As you grow spiritually, you develop a deep-rooted commitment to live this righteous life and reach out to spend counteract the dark forces in this world. As you grow, you develop for others. As you experience more of God, His very nature, it affects and influences the lives of others. It draws those around you to desire to experience the same intimacy and connection with Jesus.

Once the decision has been made to renew the mind from a sin consciousness and to transform a way of thinking to seek His righteousness (His way of doing and being right), this way of life manifests itself through the very works that you do. By knowing who you are in Christ, it opens the door to your understanding that works are not required for your position of righteousness but required for the benefits or rewards that are made available by God. It's a way of life! It's obtained by FAITH! And, because of who you are, you should have a lifestyle of doing good works. In other words, you inherently have the heart to do the works of GOD; good works. Ephesians 2:10 (GOD's Word Translation) says, *"God has made us what we are. He has created us in Christ Jesus to live lives filled with good works that he has prepared for us to do"*. The Amplified Bible says it this way, *"For we are God's [own] handiwork (His workmanship), recreated in Christ Jesus, [born anew] that we may do those good works which God predestined (planned beforehand) for us [taking paths which He prepared ahead of time], that we should walk in them [living the good life which He prearranged and made ready for us to live]"*.

It's essential, as a child of God, that you know and understand that at the born-again experience you were made the righteousness of God. Second Corinthians 5:21 states, *"For He made Him who knew no sin to be sin for us, that we might become the righteousness of God in Him."* However, you must receive this gift of grace by faith. Just as salvation, healing, peace, prosperity, etc. is received by faith, so must righteousness. Take it, by faith! Receive it, by faith! And, live it in fullness and walk it out, by faith! Paul says in Romans 3:21-22, *"But now the righteousness of God apart from the law is revealed, being witnessed by the Law and the Prophets, even the righteousness of God, through faith in Jesus Christ, to all and on all who believe. For there is no difference;"*

Abraham demonstrated this very kind of faith. God made a covenant promise to Abraham, that he would be the father of many nations. Despite the circumstances that faced him: his age, Sarah's age, the deadness of Sarah's womb and the ridicule and doubt of those around him, Abraham remained in faith and didn't waver. The Bible declares that the fulfillment of this promise to Abraham wasn't through the law, but the righteousness of faith. Abraham had complete confidence that God was faithful and would perform what He had promised. Simply put, Abraham believed God! Romans 4:16 says it this way, *"Therefore it is of faith that it might be according to grace, so that the promise might be sure to all the seed, not only to those who are of the law but also to those who are of the faith of Abraham, who is the father of us all"*.

A daily affirmation that you are the righteousness of God and that it is legally yours dispels the voice of a sin consciousness that tries to remind or keep you focused on missing the mark yesterday, a week ago or ten years ago.

Holy Spirit confirms with your spirit and continually reminds you of your true nature in Christ. Knowing who you are in Christ encourages you to walk confidently in this righteousness. You have greater peace and a greater sense of joy and happiness in your life. Righteousness makes it possible for you to impact the lives of people in a greater way as a result of you being right and having a right position with God. It's an outward demonstration of the righteousness of God within. Just as a certain fashionable brand of clothing or shoe is recognized by a popular company logo, you too are known or identified by the fruit that you

> *As the righteousness of God, your life becomes an example to the world.*

produce. This fruit serves as a clear indication to the world that you are not only a child of God, but you represent the very heart and nature of God. Your boldness and confidence to do what's right and carry out God's plan increases the expression of His love and divine nature in the Earth. It proclaims to the world that God is RIGHTEOUS, JUST and HE is LOVE!

As trees of righteousness, you are planted with a firm resolution to persistently operate in ways of God. Just as trees are planted and not moved, you too should be planted and not be moved. Circumstances, situations, feelings or others shouldn't move you from doing and being right. In those times, where you need support and strength, just as the Redwood draws from the roots of surrounding trees, you too should draw from your chief source; Jesus, and fellow Believers in faith.

So, each day declare that you are a new creation in Christ Jesus and you have the very nature of God; His righteousness!

SHOUT OUT LOUD:

> "I AM A NEW CREATION IN CHRIST JESUS!
> "I AM A CHILD OF GOD!"
> "I AM HIS WORKMANSHIP!"
> "RIGHTEOUSNESS IS WHO I AM!"
> "RIGHTEOUSNESS IS WHAT I DO!"
> "I AM THE RIGHTEOUSNESS OF GOD IN CHRIST JESUS!"

My Hope for You

Friend, I hope that you enjoyed this journey INWARD as you came to Understand Your True Nature in Christ.

If you have not received this wonderful salvation experience, I would like to invite you to make it a reality now. Pray the following prayer:

Heavenly Father, I come to you in the Name of Your Son Jesus Christ. You said in Your Word that whosoever should call upon the name of the Lord shall be saved. (Romans 10:13) Father, I am calling on Jesus right now. I believe He died on the cross for my sins that He was raised from the dead on the third day, and He's alive right now. Lord Jesus, I am asking You now, come into my heart. Live your life in me and through me. I repent of my sins and surrender myself totally and completely to you. Heavenly Father, by faith I now confess Jesus Christ as my new Lord and from this day forward, I dedicate my life to serving Him, In Jesus Name! Amen.

Let me be the first to welcome you to the body of Christ. Your next step is to find a bible believing, bible teaching local church to attend as it is important that you learn more about your new nature in Christ. If I can assist you in any way, please visit www.fccintl.org and fill out an information form located on the Contact Us page.

God bless!

136